HOLDING FAST

HOLDING FAST

RESILIENCE AND CIVIC ENGAGEMENT
AMONG LATINO IMMIGRANTS

James A. McCann and Michael Jones-Correa

Russell Sage Foundation   NEW YORK

LIBRARY OF CONGRESS
CATALOGING-IN-PUBLICATION DATA
Names: McCann, James A., 1962- author. | Jones-Correa, Michael, 1965- author. | Russell Sage Foundation, issuing body.
Title: Holding fast : resilience and civic engagement among Latino immigrants / James A. McCann, Michael Jones-Correa.
Other titles: Resilience and civic engagement among Latino immigrants
Description: New York, New York : Russell Sage Foundation, [2020] | Includes bibliographical references and index. | Summary: "Drawing primarily from an original longitudinal survey of Latino immigrants that spanned a pivotal and tumultuous year in U.S. politics—from the summer of 2016 through the summer of 2017, as Trump consolidated his position as the Republican nominee for President, was elected to the presidency, and took office—this book charts patterns of civic resilience or withdrawal among these foreign-born residents, both citizens and noncitizens. Despite the rhetoric and policy threat of Trump's candidacy and presidency, the evidence indicates far more civic resilience among Latino immigrants than withdrawal. Latino immigrants, who are part of the largest minority group in the United States and, together with their children, a substantial portion of the American electorate, will be increasingly important players in American politics, as the evidence in this volume suggests. The conclusion the authors draw is one of immigrants' civic resilience in the face of communal threat—of immigrants holding fast"—Provided by publisher.
Identifiers: LCCN 2020024573 (print) | LCCN 2020024574 (ebook) | ISBN 9780871545695 (paperback ; alk. paper) | ISBN 9781610448925 (ebook)
Subjects: LCSH: Hispanic Americans—Politics and government—21st century. Latin Americans—United States—Politics and government—21st century. Immigrants—United States—Politics and government—21st century. | Hispanic Americans—Political activity—History—21st century. | Latin Americans—Political activity—United States—History—21st century. | Immigrants—Political activity—United States—History—21st century. | United States—Emigration and immigration—Political aspects. | United States—Politics and government—2017-
Classification: LCC E184.S75 M399 2020 (print) | LCC E184.S75 (ebook) | DDC 305.868/073—dc23
LC record available at https://lccn.loc.gov/2020024573
LC ebook record available at https://lccn.loc.gov/2020024574

Text design by Matthew T. Avery.

RUSSELL SAGE FOUNDATION
112 East 64th Street,
New York, New York 10065
10 9 8 7 6 5 4 3 2 1

CONTENTS

LIST OF ILLUSTRATIONS

ABOUT THE AUTHORS

JAMES A. MCCANN is Professor of Political Science at Purdue University.

MICHAEL JONES-CORREA is President's Distinguished Professor of Political Science at the University of Pennsylvania.

ACKNOWLEDGMENTS

As with most ambitious research projects, the end point to this book is quite different from its beginning. Early in 2016, we put together a proposal focusing on immigrants' engagement with American politics, and in particular on the role of campaigns as "teaching moments" about democracy for immigrants in the process of becoming both political actors and citizens. The project built on our experience in fielding the 2012 Latino Immigrant National Election Study (LINES), which culminated in a collection of articles based on this data set by leading scholars in the fields of immigration, ethnic politics, and public opinion published in *RSF: The Russell Sage Foundation Journal of the Social Sciences* (DOI to our introduction to the issue: 10.7758 /RSF.2016.2.3.01, available at https://www.rsfjournal.org/content/2/3). In what we thought of as our follow-up study in 2016, we wanted to explore the attitudes and involvement of the foreign-born during periods of intense political campaigning and compare their political engagement to that of native-born citizens, using a panel study design in which respondents would be interviewed over two waves, one before and one after the November elections.

Even as we were drumming up support for this research, it was clear that the 2016 election cycle was shaping up to be quite different from previous ones. Former senator Hillary Clinton, who had the Democratic establishment's support, was in a hard-fought nomination battle with Senator Bernie Sanders, while on the Republican side an unprecedented field of eighteen candidates had been in the running for the party's nomination, with seven still in consideration as of February. Going into the spring, it was clear the likely leading candidate was New York City real estate tycoon Donald Trump, who had launched his campaign with invective targeting Mexican immigrants and who built his campaign on a slogan of "build the wall," chanted in unison by thousands of supporters at his raucous campaign rallies. Trump's campaign added another twist to our study: we could now see not only how immigrants learned about democratic politics and engagement as campaigns reached out to them (or did not), but also how immigrants reacted as a leading candidate, and then the nominee, of one of the nation's two major parties targeted immigrants with negative messaging about their place in American society.

By then, the project had received support from the Russell Sage Foundation (award 93-16-11) to move ahead, and we fielded the first wave of our panel study in the late summer of 2016, not long before the elections, and a second wave of the survey, following many of the same respondents, shortly after the election in November through mid-January 2017. Like many other observers, we were surprised by the outcome of the 2016 election. We also realized that we were in a unique position to trace not only the effects of the 2016 campaign on the political views of immigrant voters, but to see how Trump's candidacy, his election, and his transition to the presidency would shape Latino immigrants' opinions, attitudes, and behavior in this new era of resurgent American nativism. In particular, both before and after the election there was a good deal of commentary about Trump's negative impacts on Latino immigrants; the pervasive narrative was one of fear and withdrawal. What, we wondered, would be the effect of Trump's election as president on Latino immigrants' political engagement? Would it send immigrants underground to wait out the anti-immigrant storm around them, or would they hold fast and stand firm, galvanized by the election to raise their voices higher? With these questions in mind, we scrambled to put together funding for a third wave of the panel study, which was fielded in the summer of 2017, approximately six months after President Trump was sworn into office.

We are immensely grateful to the foundations and universities that have made possible the line of inquiry we began with the 2012 LINES and continued into the 2016–2017 LINES. The Russell Sage Foundation (award 88-13-03) and the Carnegie Corporation of

New York (award 13015) were the principal backers of the earlier study; we wish in particular to thank Aixa Cintrón-Velez of the Russell Sage Foundation and Geri Mannion of the Carnegie Corporation for their wise counsel, constructive criticism, and unstinting support throughout. The Russell Sage Foundation was the primary funder of the 2016–2017 LINES, with Aixa again providing invaluable assistance. We are indebted to our universities for their support as well: we received research grants from Purdue University (McCann), Cornell University, and the University of Pennsylvania (Jones-Correa) that, in particular, enabled us to conduct the third wave of the study. At Purdue, Eliza Osorio Castro provided helpful research assistance, and McCann is grateful for a research fellowship appointment with the Purdue University College of Liberal Arts Center for Social Sciences in the spring of 2018. At the University of Pennsylvania, Katherine Fink and Christine Sommerville helped as research assistants as well.

A very preliminary version of the argument presented here was delivered at the American Political Science Association's annual conference in San Francisco in 2017. We would like to thank the participants at our panel discussion, in particular Alexandra Filindra, Louis DeSipio, and Jacqueline Chattopadhyay, for their very helpful comments and feedback. The association's Section on Race, Ethnicity, and Politics gave this initial write-up of our findings its award for Best Paper Presented at the 2017 Meeting, which reinforced our sense that perhaps we were on to something.

A very special thanks goes to Suzanne Nichols, the director of publications at the Russell Sage Foundation. This book might well not have happened, and certainly would not have come together as *quickly*, without her unwavering belief in the project and encouragement. Our gratitude cannot be overstated. Finally, our heartfelt thanks go to our spouses and families. Ann and Ria in particular were the best of sounding boards at every stage of this project—this in addition to all the other ways they show their love and support. We dedicate this book to them.

INTRODUCTION 1

AN EMERGING BIPARTISAN CONSENSUS
ON IMMIGRATION IS DISRUPTED

During the 2016 presidential election, the celebrity billionaire Donald Trump charged that sinister forces were threatening the United States—forces that threatened to undermine the U.S. economy and wipe out traditional American culture. Dangers such as these, Trump maintained, called for strong countermeasures so that the United States could be made "great again." Styling himself as a one-of-a-kind disrupter, the Republican standard-bearer pursued a mode of campaigning pledging to overturn a multitude of policies, executive orders, and tacit agreements on trade, foreign policy, environmental pollution, education, and immigration—especially immigration, which is the focus of this book. Indeed, in the seventy-three formal campaign speeches that Trump delivered from the time of his announcement to the day of the 2016 election, no subject came up as frequently as immigration, and the vast majority of references were condemnatory.[1] This positioning on immigration stood in marked contrast to that of Hillary Clinton and several of Trump's rivals for the Republican presidential nomination.[2] Although various officials and activists in the Republican Party over the last several decades have often pushed for lower levels of immigration, stricter enforcement of immigration policies, and stepped-up deportations of unauthorized immigrants, Republican presidential nominees immediately prior to Trump were not as much in this mold.[3] Mitt Romney, John McCain, George W. Bush—none made anti-immigrant nativism a central theme of his campaign. Mitt Romney certainly took positions in 2012, such as the desirability for undocumented immigrants to "self-deport," that were less supportive of immigration in comparison to John McCain in 2008 and George W. Bush in 2000 and 2004. Romney did not, however, lead with this issue.[4] Trump's stances consequently represented an appreciable break with precedent. What effect has this break had on those who have been the target of Trump's rhetoric—immigrants themselves? This question is the central focus of this book.

Since Donald Trump became president, academics, journalists, and news commentators have sought to track the extent of this disruption and the potential impact of the Trump administration on public opinion, political involvement, party competition, and the overall workings of American democracy.[5] We aim to add to this important conversation through a close examination of how Latino immigrants—a group that is vulnerable in many respects and has been frequently targeted by the White House and its affiliates—are faring. Have the stressors and disappointments of the Trump era undermined their trajectories of political inclusion?

Drawing primarily from an original longitudinal survey of Latino immigrants that spanned a pivotal and tumultuous year in U.S. politics—from the summer of 2016 through the summer of 2017, as Trump consolidated his position as the Republican nominee for president, was elected to the presidency, and took office—this book charts patterns of civic resilience or withdrawal among these foreign-born residents, both citizens and noncitizens. Over the next several chapters we show that despite the rhetoric and policy threat of Trump's candidacy and presidency, the evidence indicates far more civic resilience than withdrawal among Latino immigrants.

This narrative of resilience was by no means immediately obvious following the 2016 elections. To anticipate some of our central findings, we show that after the election immigrants from Latin America signaled significant pessimism about the future direction of the country. Moreover, among Latino immigrants who were concerned about where the country was heading, there was a decline as well in their belief that government was truly looking out for their interests. Immigrants, and particularly immigrants from Latin America, had been repeatedly targeted by the Republican candidate as a source of corruption and criminality, and so it is not surprising that Trump's election in 2016 would have triggered a wave of pessimism and concern. More vulnerable immigrants expressed the most disquiet: immigrants who worried that a friend or family member would be deported, for instance, were significantly less trusting of governing institutions than they had been prior to the 2016 elections. In short, the increased stress introduced by the 2016 elections—reflected in concerns about the country and its leadership and concerns about the well-being of those within immigrants' social networks—led immigrants to question their faith in American government.

What is more surprising is the finding that the increased civic stress related to fears of deportation, financial woes, misgivings about the direction of the country, and the actions of Donald Trump did not seem to lead immigrants to "exit" from U.S. civic life. The period around the 2016 elections, for example, did not increase doubts among Latin American immigrants about remaining in the United States over the long run—even among the overwhelming majority of those who were not U.S. citizens, or who were in the country without authorization. Nor did it lead immigrants to follow a"softer" kind of exiting in the form of psychological estrangement from American society—trusting Americans less, or feeling less of an emotional attachment to the country. These findings hold true even accounting for the state contexts in which immigrants lived— that is, whether these contexts were more or less accommodating to undocumented residents—and immigrants' own legal status, national origin, and time spent in the United States. In short, even while Latino immigrants became more pessimistic about the direction of the country and the country's governing institutions following the 2016 elections, there is no evidence that they pulled back from U.S. society. Our findings suggest that within the Latino immigrant community, even among those in the country without papers, attachments to the United States ran deep.

Perhaps more surprising is that even with the rise in pessimism about the direction of the country and the decline of faith in government, Latin American immigrants showed no signs of withdrawing from broader civic engagement. There was an outpouring of civic protest and engagement more generally following the 2016 elections, and we find that immigrant voices followed suit, despite the arguably higher costs of participation for many immigrants following Trump's election, with his administration's renewed focus on immigration enforcement. One in five immigrants in our study participated in protest activity following the 2016 elections, for example. In addition, the likelihood of turning out for a protest rally was nearly ten points higher for immigrants who felt strong negative emotions about Trump, and over ten points higher for those concerned that a friend or family member would be deported. Nor did participating in protests "crowd out" other forms of political engagement: on the contrary, we find that attending an immigrant rights protest was positively—not negatively—correlated with other participation measures. For Latino immigrants, protest involvement and conventional participation seemed to be mutually reinforcing.

The conclusion we draw is that immigrants are holding fast, maintaining civic resilience even in the face of communal threat. This finding offers the political parties both promise and peril. The promise lies in the fact that these Latino immigrants, who are part of the largest minority group in the United States and, together with their children, a substantial portion of the American electorate, will be increasingly important players in American politics, as the evidence in this volume suggests. Immigrants can be courted by both Democrats and Republicans, and indeed, up until the 2016 elections, both political parties were reaching out to this potential electorate. After 2016, however, the Republican Party discarded the lessons supposedly learned after their loss in the 2012 elections and shifted to a narrower strategic focus on the mobilization of white voters. In the face of the continuing mobilization of new immigrant political actors—reflected, for example, in higher turnout rates in the 2018 midterms—this strategy is indeed a perilous one.

This introductory chapter sets the stage for our analysis by first providing an overview of the recent wave of migrant settlement in the United States. It then considers partisan positioning around "immigration" amid this influx of newcomers. In the years leading up to the 2016 elections, a bipartisan consensus on immigration policy reform appeared to be emerging. This fledgling consensus, however, proved to be fragile, unrealistic, and short-lived.

The New Immigration

The longtime public characterization of the United States as a nation of immigrants, often accompanied by a good deal of civic pride, has fallen short of a more complex reality, but rhetorically at least it has emphasized that strangers are to be welcomed and diversity widely celebrated. When they are asked about the qualities that make someone a "true American," there is a strong consensus among U.S. citizens that respecting other people's cultural differences, seeing individuals from all backgrounds as American, and carrying on the language and traditions of one's ancestors are key defining elements.[6] Over the last decades government officials from the right, left, and center have routinely trumpeted similar sentiments. By way of illustration, consider these passages from State of the Union addresses delivered by four very different chief executives over nearly half a century:

"It is imperative that our immigration policy be in the finest American tradition of providing a haven for oppressed peoples and fully in accord with our obligation as a leader of the free world" (Dwight Eisenhower, 1961).

"Immigrants to this country always contribute more toward making our country stronger than they ever take from the system. I am confident that the newest arrivals to our country will carry on this tradition" (Jimmy Carter, 1981).

"Our nation is the enduring dream of every immigrant who ever set foot on these shores, and the millions still struggling to be free. This nation, this idea called America was and always will be a new world, our new world" (G. H. W. Bush, 1990).

"We need to uphold the great tradition of the melting pot that welcomes and assimilates new arrivals" (G. W. Bush, 2007).

Presidents of both parties have consistently celebrated the core contributions of immigration to the American experiment.

Even with increasing disagreement about the direction of U.S. immigration policy, Americans are still largely supportive of the principle of taking in migrants from abroad who have been exploited or are simply searching for a better life. Yet at the same time, concerns about whether immigrants can ever truly be incorporated into the economic, social, and civic life of the country also run deep in the American psyche. When the country was founded in the late eighteenth century, the terms "race," "people," and "nation" were used interchangeably in everyday discourse. For many Americans, settlers from abroad represented a threat to national unity and purpose. The pseudo-scientific claims of social Darwinism in the late nineteenth and early twentieth centuries, which applied the concept of "survival of the fittest" to all manner of social and ethnic groups, exacerbated concerns in many circles about national integrity.[7] An excerpt from another State of the Union address, given by Theodore Roosevelt in 1905, trenchantly captures this mindset. At a time when approximately one out of seven residents of the United States was foreign-born, the president told Congress that "we cannot have too much immigration of the right sort and we should have none whatever of the wrong sort. . . . The laws now existing for the exclusion of undesirable immigrants should be strengthened." Roosevelt went on in his address to put a finer distinction on his understanding of the "wrong sort" of immigrants. These were, he believed, prospective settlers who would be disorderly, weak, lazy, or immoral, would lower the standard of living for native-born workers, or would espouse ideologies, such as anarchism, that were incompatible with American political ideals.

Our own era has seen a rise in migrant settlement that is comparable to that in Theodore Roosevelt's day. Over the last fifty years, the percentage of foreign-born in the United States has risen from a low of less than 4 percent in 1970 to almost 15 percent in 2020. Today nearly 45 million people living in the United States—or just under one in seven of all residents—are foreign-born. Most of these immigrants have formal legal standing to be in the country: 45 percent are naturalized citizens, and 32 percent are legal permanent or temporary residents. The remaining 23 percent—approximately one out of four of the foreign-born—lack authorization to reside in the country, either because they settled without "inspection" by government officials or they overstayed an entry visa.[8] Unlike in earlier periods of American history, settlers in this latest wave have come primarily from Latin America and Asia rather than Europe. Mexicans, by far the largest national-origin group, comprise more than one-quarter of all immigrants and a majority of those from Latin America, although overall migration from Mexico has peaked and the largest immigrant stream is now from Asia. Such settlement has added immeasurably to cultural diversity across the United States. It is now common for native-born Americans to hear languages other than English when shopping, pumping gas, or relaxing in their local park.

As in the past, worries are frequently voiced about whether the "right" kinds of immigrants are entering the United States, and whether the foreign-born population is altogether too large. Contemporary public opinion polls present a jumble of competing beliefs and attitudes about immigrants and immigration. Perhaps as many as half of all those who believe that one should respect cultural differences and view others as "American" regardless of ethnic heritage simultaneously doubt whether anyone born outside of the United States can ever actually become a "true American."[9] Over the last twenty years, the public has been nearly evenly split on whether immigrants "pay their fair share of taxes" and on whether they "cost taxpayers too much," and there are high levels of anxiety about potential job losses due to immigration. At the same time, most Americans these days would agree that immigration on balance is a good thing for the country and that unauthorized immigrants should not be summarily deported.[10] In short, public opinion, while often sympathetic to immigrants, is far from coalescing around a single set of policies about immigration.

Asymmetric Partisan Polarization

These conflicting views on immigrants and immigration have come to be reflected over the years in the positioning and branding of the two major American political parties. The official platforms of the Democratic Party have long honored immigrant contributions to the United States and multiculturalism. The Democratic platform from 2012, for instance, proclaimed that "the story of the United States would not be possible without the generations of immigrants who have strengthened our country and contributed to our economy." Similar sentiments appeared in platforms from the 1980s, 1990s, and early 2000s. Republican Party platforms, in contrast, have tended to emphasize the potential downside of immigration, particularly the settlement of undocumented immigrants—threats to national security, the depression of wages for native-born workers, and challenges to traditional American values. In 1988, for example, the Republican platform insisted "upon our country's absolute right to control its borders." A generation later, in 2012, the party declared that, "in an age of terrorism, drug cartels, human trafficking, and criminal gangs, the presence of millions of unidentified persons in the country poses grave risks." The Republicans that year further advocated the adoption of English as the "official language" of the United States and, in an echo of Theodore Roosevelt's remark about the "right" and "wrong" sort of immigration, called for more highly educated immigrants to be admitted.

Such partisan polarization is of course hardly unique to policies concerning immigration. But the positioning of the parties on immigration may be distinctive in comparison to various other policy areas in that polarization in this instance is asymmetric. That is, the "anti-immigrant" disposition of rank-and-file Republican partisans has been more pronounced over the years than the more favorable views of the Democrats.[11] This asymmetry stands out clearly in surveys of party activists. The men and women who voluntarily take part in partisan caucuses, conventions, and campaigns help to establish the image of their party in the eyes of the general public. They are in effect the living embodiment of party platforms. As such, data on how activists position themselves on issues can tell us much about policymaking priorities and the contours of partisan polarization.

By way of illustration, consider how Republican and Democratic activists from three states (Iowa, Michigan, and Virginia) who had attended local party caucus meetings responded in 1996—at the height of a period of debates to restrict immigration and harden the U.S. border with Mexico—to a survey item asking whether they would support or oppose limits on immigration to the United States. As is clear in figure 1.1, among Republicans, nearly three-fourths favored limiting immigration, with 31 percent expressing the strongest support for this policy. Only a small minority of Republicans opposed limits. For their part, Democratic activists were significantly less supportive of enacting limits—just 43 percent took this position. Yet while more Democrats opposed limits on immigration than favored them, the distribution of opinions here was far less lopsided than for Republicans. The two partisan camps voiced markedly different stances on the whole, but Republicans were more extreme and unified in their positions than Democrats.

Figure 1.1 *"Do You Favor or Oppose Placing Stricter Limits on the Number of Immigrants Allowed into This Country?": Preferences of Party Activists Who Attended Local Caucuses in Three States in 1996*

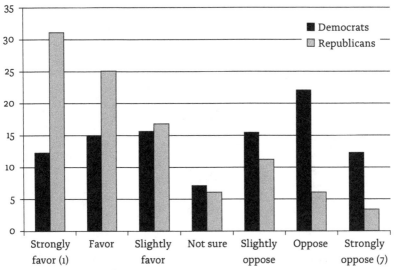

Source: Abramowitz et al. 2001.

Note: Party activists attended local caucuses in Iowa, Michigan, and Virginia. For Democrats, N = 375, mean = 4.14, and standard deviation = 2.00; for Republicans, N = 179, mean = 2.73, and standard deviation = 1.74. Levine's test for equality of variances = 17.2 ($p < .001$); t-test for equality of means (equal variances not assumed) = 8.5 ($p < .001$).

Similar patterns emerged ten years later in the 2006 Cooperative Congressional Election Study, a large online survey that netted sizable groups of engaged partisans—that is, Republicans and Democrats who strongly identified with their party, made financial contributions to campaigns, and persuaded friends and family members to back particular candidates. The people taking part in the Cooperative Congressional Election Study were not asked whether levels of immigration to the United States should be decreased, but they did express opinions on policies toward immigrants who were currently living in the country without authorization. They were asked: Should government agencies step up enforcement, so that greater numbers of these immigrants are deported? Or should a pathway to citizenship be extended to the undocumented? At the time of the survey, leading immigration bills in the U.S. House of

Figure 1.2 *Preferences of Party Activists Concerning Immigration Policy Reform, 2006*

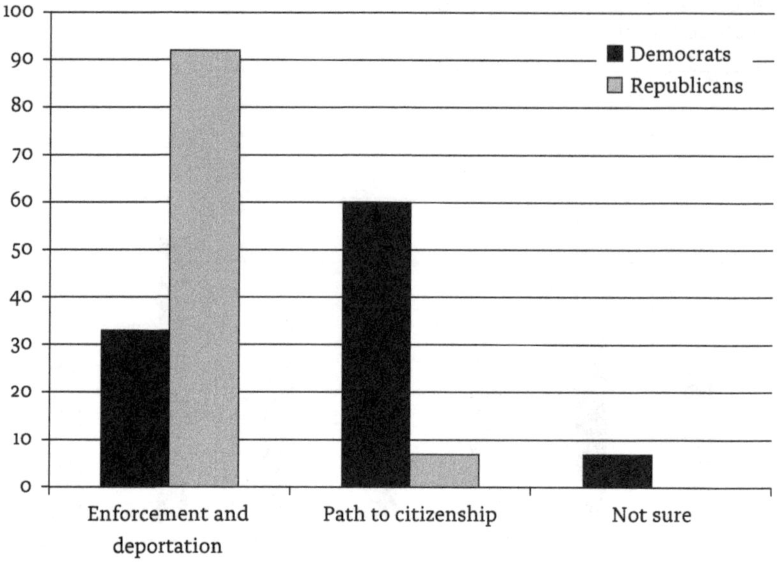

Source: Ansolabehere 2012.

Note: The question asked whether the reform priority should be "a path to citizenship for illegal immigrants" or "stricter enforcement and deportation of undocumented aliens." Respondents were strong partisans who reported donating to campaigns and persuading others to support particular candidates in the 2006 election cycle. N = 855 (Democrats) and 782 (Republicans). χ^2_2 = 602 ($p < .001$).

Representatives emphasized enforcement and deportation, while the discussion in the Senate focused on broadening access to naturalization for unauthorized immigrants. How did Democratic and Republican activists come down on this question?

The breakdown of opinions shown in figure 1.2 provides another picture of asymmetric party positioning in the years leading up to Trump's presidential bid. Politically engaged Republicans were essentially of one mind: all but a handful wished to see stronger enforcement of immigration laws and more deportations.[12] Democratic campaign activists, on the other hand, generally fell on the side of expanding naturalization opportunities for undocumented immigrants. As early as 2006, then, partisan polarization was quite apparent. Yet Democrats were definitely not uniform in their preferences—certainly not as unified or as intensely focused on this issue as deeply engaged Republicans.

An Attempt to Redirect the Republicans Fails

In principle, political party activists giving clear signals about their stances on a major issue could be taken as a virtue. From the standpoint of a voter attempting to weigh the pros and cons of Democrats versus Republicans, uncertainties about where a party truly stands can make the task of choosing between candidates difficult. From the vantage point of many Republican leaders, however, the widespread perception in the early 2000s that their party stood in opposition to cultural diversity and wished to manage undocumented immigrants with a heavy hand was a liability, at least in national elections. Polls conducted during that period showed that, on immigration issues, Americans were generally closer to the positions espoused by Democratic caucus attendees in 1996 and campaign activists in 2006: they were broadly supportive of immigration and immigrant rights, but not stridently so.

Take, for example, some of the findings from the American National Election Studies (ANES) conducted in 2004, 2008, and 2012. In these surveys, study participants indicated whether they wished to see immigration levels increased, decreased, or left the same. Across these three very different national election cycles, there was striking consistency in responses: 52 to 55 percent of the public over this period either were satisfied with current levels of immigration or wanted to see more immigrant settlement.[13] The number of Americans preferring substantially less migration—the prevailing attitude among Republican activists—never rose beyond one out of four. Along similar lines, between 2006 and 2011 the Gallup survey organization repeatedly queried Americans about whether the government should (a) "deport all illegal immigrants," (b) "allow illegal immigrants to remain in the United States in order to work," or (c) "allow illegal immigrants to remain in the United States and become U.S. citizens, but only if they meet certain requirements over a period of time." Preferences in this case were also consistent over time: nearly two-thirds of the public supported giving the undocumented a path to citizenship; only one in five Americans favored deportation.[14]

In the aftermath of the 2012 presidential election, it appeared to Reince Priebus, chairman of the Republican National Committee (RNC), and other key officials in the party that the Republicans might have painted themselves into a corner on issues related to immigration, race, ethnicity, and multiculturalism. Former Massachusetts governor Mitt Romney, the party's nominee for president that year, had lost decisively to Barack Obama, a failure that followed losses in the presidential elections of 2008, 1996, and 1992, and a loss of the popular vote in 2000. Priebus and other Republican leaders recognized that the demographic makeup of the country was changing rapidly, and they feared that anti-immigrant stances were driving away voters who might otherwise support the party because of its conservative positions on, say, taxes, education, foreign policy, and abortion.

Postmortem reflections such as these about what went wrong for the Republicans in 2012 highlighted a long-standing divide within the party—a divide between ideologically minded rank-and-file partisans and more pragmatic Republicans in leadership positions who saw their central mission as winning elections. In his classic work *An Economic Theory of Democracy*, the Brookings Institution scholar Anthony Downs posited that "parties formulate policies in order to win elections, rather than win elections in order to formulate policies."[15] This sweeping theoretical claim has been widely debated in both academic venues and partisan strategy sessions. A good many Democrats and Republicans would surely bristle at the notion that policy commitments can be or should be switched on and off depending on the winds of public opinion before an election. In addition, voters themselves are likely to look down on such a seeming lack of integrity. Downs's basic premise, however, is beyond dispute. Partisan leaders in any democracy must necessarily strive to convey the most inviting sets of policies and programs to the electorate, even if this means dialing back or renouncing some of their previous positions. Parties that cannot win major elections have no choice but to try to rebrand themselves. Otherwise, they risk drifting into oblivion.

With these strategic considerations as a backdrop, the Republicans commissioned the "Growth and Opportunity Project" in December 2012. The central mission of this initiative was to move the party toward the mainstream of American public opinion on issues related to immigration and ethnic diversity so as to improve its chances in future presidential elections. As stated in the first report from this project: "Public perception of the Party is at record lows. Young voters are increasingly rolling their eyes at what the Party represents, and many minorities wrongly think that Republicans do not like them or want them in the country."[16] In addition to Reince Priebus, the other coordinators of this initiative included a former RNC chairman, several high-ranking officials from the Reagan, G. H. W. Bush, and G. W. Bush administrations, and the chair of the Romney presidential campaign in Puerto Rico. This body was careful to stress that its mandate did not include policy development. Nevertheless, the project report called on Republicans at all levels to "embrace and champion comprehensive immigration reform. If we do not, our Party's appeal will continue to shrink to its core constituencies only. We also believe that comprehensive immigration reform is consistent with Republican economic policies that promote job growth and opportunity for all."[17] The phrase "comprehensive immigration reform" was not clearly defined in the document, but it was generally understood to include continuing legal channels for immigration while making the rules for granting visas more business-friendly, allowing many current undocumented immigrants to remain in the United States, and increasing surveillance and security both in the interior of the country and along its borders.

The leaders of the Growth and Opportunity Project wrote that this recommendation emerged from extensive data-gathering from more than fifty focus group meetings with local Republican leaders throughout the country, online surveys that polled more than thirty-six thousand Americans, and conference calls with Republican Party officials from Asian American and Latino communities, among other activities. The final report on the project in March 2015 highlighted the positive example of the party's strategic overtures to ethnic minority communities (Latinos, African Americans, and Asian Americans), with more than 1.6 million minority voters contacted during the 2014 midterm elections. This report also identified senior-level advisory councils within the party to coordinate outreach to minority-serving groups such as the NAACP, the National Association of Latino Elected and Appointed Officials, and the National Urban League Conference.

Chairman Priebus and the other national party leaders driving this initiative no doubt had hopes that they could reorient the

Republicans in advance of the 2016 presidential contest, steering the nomination toward a candidate with conservative credentials in matters of economic and foreign policy but without a history of antagonizing immigrants and minority voters. In previous election cycles since the 1980s, both Republican and Democratic elites had managed to coordinate candidate selection months in advance of the presidential primaries and caucuses. To be sure, a presidential aspirant had to earn his or her nomination by winning these primaries and caucuses, thereby accruing delegates for the national party convention. Yet the field of serious contenders had generally been winnowed down considerably by the start of the election year. Well before the first-in-the-nation Iowa caucuses in January or February, key interest groups making up a major party coalition, along with partisan fundraisers, consultants, and officeholders, would signal to one another which candidates were most attractive and electable. Signaling of this sort has been dubbed the "invisible" primary.[18] Candidates who performed well in this invisible primary generally had a leg up in the actual primaries and caucuses.

If the 2016 nomination contest had followed in this mold, the intraparty networking that was part of the Republican National Committee's Growth and Opportunity Project could have helped anoint a standard-bearer who would have been more popular among ethnic voters. Former Florida governor Jeb Bush would have been a natural choice for these Republican insiders. Bush had not only prior executive experience and a last name with near-universal recognition but also unassailable credentials as a conservative, one who also happened to speak fluent Spanish and had recently published a book calling for bipartisan immigration policy reform that would extend special residency papers to unauthorized immigrants.[19]

Republican coordination in advance of the 2016 primaries, however, proved to be difficult. Sensing an opportunity to retake the White House after eight years under President Obama, more than a dozen Republican candidates were actively campaigning for the presidency at the time of the Iowa caucuses. Several of these contenders—Senator Marco Rubio of Florida and Governor John Kasich of Ohio being among the most prominent—had taken relatively moderate stands on immigration that resonated with the goals of the Growth and Opportunity Project. Others, including

Senator Ted Cruz from Texas, former governor Mike Huckabee of Arkansas, former senator Rick Santorum of Pennsylvania, and of course Donald Trump, staked out much more restrictive immigration policies. In this crowded field, no uniquely compelling front-runner emerged for elite Republican insiders during the invisible primary.

This failure to coordinate made the presidential nomination decision more of a bottom-up than a top-down affair. Any candidate who could mobilize a committed personal following among the different rank-and-file constituencies within the party stood to gain traction. A competitive environment such as this was tailor-made for Donald Trump. Although Trump had never before run for elective office, he was well known for his outspoken views on ethnicity, race, multiculturalism, national identity, and immigration. He had made his first foray into national politics only a few years earlier, when he became the leading figure in the United States to question whether Barack Obama was a natural-born citizen. In his campaign announcement speech in June 2015, Trump railed against international trade treaties, Obamacare, crime, and, most vociferously, immigration, singling out Mexican immigrants in particular as a threat to public safety and security: "When Mexico sends its people, they're not sending their best. They're not sending you. They're not sending you. They're sending people that have lots of problems, and they're bringing those problems with us. They're bringing drugs. They're bringing crime. They're rapists. And some, I assume, are good people."[20] John Sides, Michael Tesler, and Lynn Vavreck show that Trump's distinctive commingling of economic and cultural grievances, and particularly his hawkish views on migration, appealed to a significant portion of the party's rank-and-file base—a cohort that had been visible for years before the billionaire declared his candidacy. As these authors put it, Trump "simply hunted where the ducks are" better than any of his rivals.[21] In a divided primary winning with a plurality of support was sufficient.

Over the objections of party insiders, Trump clenched the nomination in early May 2016, though his vote tally across all of the Republican caucuses and primaries totaled only 45 percent. The party generally came together to support its presidential nominee during the fall general election campaign. Trump disregarded the "move-to-the-center" strategy underlying the Republican National

Committee's Growth and Opportunity Project. As noted earlier, immigration was a persistent theme in Trump's campaign speeches. For every good thing the candidate said about immigrants, he made more than six other comments that were disparaging.[22] A speech he delivered in Arizona on August 31, 2016, summed up the candidate's ambitious anti-immigrant platform. This agenda included the hiring of more agents for U.S. Immigration and Customs Enforcement (ICE), a crackdown on "sanctuary" cities, termination of an Obama-era executive order that deferred the deportation of immigrants who had come to the country as children without papers, a reduction in legal migration, and the construction of an "impenetrable" wall along the two-thousand-mile U.S.-Mexico border.

With the support of a highly motivated base, Donald Trump, of course, won the presidency that fall, an outcome that few foresaw. Trump won in the electoral college despite findings in the 2016 American National Election Study that just one-quarter of the voters who reported backing the Republican nominee wished to see all unauthorized immigrants declared felons and deported, and fewer than half were strongly in favor of building a wall between the country and Mexico or substantially reducing levels of immigration. It would therefore be a misreading of the election results to suggest that the voting bloc that propelled Trump to an electoral college victory over the Democratic nominee, Hillary Clinton, was foursquare behind his reactionary stances on immigration policies. There is still much to learn about the forces that led to the outcome of this race. Among the most commonly cited factors for the Republican win are last-minute mobilization drives in key swing states to prompt "low-propensity" voters to turn out for Trump, Clinton's difficulties making personal connections with many Americans, a general desire in many circles for a change in direction following eight years of Democratic control of the White House, and a belief for many that the American economy was not performing as well as it could. Donald Trump's views on immigration undoubtedly pulled many voters toward the Republicans.[23] But it is also possible that, on balance, more Americans were drawn toward the Clinton campaign in opposition to these stances than were attracted to Trump because of them.

Such complexities notwithstanding, early in the transition the president-elect signaled that he would follow through on his pledges regarding immigration. Although the public was deeply divided during the elections and Trump actually lost the popular vote by a relatively wide margin, he claimed a mandate for bold action. A one-year assessment of his presidency published by the Washington-based Migration Policy Institute offers an extensive inventory of these actions.[24] Shortly after taking office, Trump sought to increase and broaden immigration enforcement, he eliminated temporary protections for noncitizens, and his administration reduced the number of refugee admissions. In September 2017, the U.S. Department of Homeland Security (DHS) rescinded the expansion of the Deferred Action for Childhood Arrivals executive order (DACA), and in September the Trump administration announced it was phasing out DACA entirely, a decision affecting hundreds of thousands of U.S. residents.[25] The White House then raised with Congress the possibility of granting some form of residency status to younger immigrants without papers in exchange for funds to construct a border wall and major new restrictions on family migration—a deal that it then walked away from.

Although the Republicans had majority control of both chambers of Congress in his first two years in office, Trump's anti-immigrant agenda met with only mixed success there at this early point in the presidential term. Several Republican lawmakers represented relatively diverse constituencies that they perceived could swing against them in future election cycles if they toed the White House line on immigration policy too closely. There was little enthusiasm within Congress to provide financial support for a wall between the United States and Mexico—a big-ticket budget item that was conservatively estimated to cost tens of billions of dollars—especially given that Trump had pledged during the presidential campaign that Mexico would pay for it. Few Republicans, however, would speak out, then or later, against the president's broad use of executive authority to place many more immigrants at risk of deportation and make it far more difficult for immigrants (documented as well as undocumented), asylum-seekers, and refugees to settle in the country.

On a rhetorical level, Trump continued as president to single out immigrants as a distinctive threat to American culture and well-being. In his first year in office, he staged nine campaign-style rallies in different parts of the country. This level of outreach to base supporters so early in the term was unprecedented in contemporary presidential politics.[26] Immigration loomed large as a prominent theme in each of these events, as it has in his social media posts.[27] Trump's tweets after taking office were unequivocal. Among the dozens of Twitter posts circulated to followers in the opening weeks of his presidency were exhortations such as "We must keep 'evil' out of the country!" (February 3, 2017) and "People pouring in. Bad!" (February 5, 2017). Trump was clearly signaling the direction he wanted his administration to take.

Immigrants Respond

To pose, once again, the central question of this book: how have immigrants themselves responded to these unprecedented White House attacks on their dignity and place in American society? In the chapters that follow, our aim is to shed fresh light not only on the attitudes and aspirations of immigrants in tumultuous times but also on the overall well-being of democracy in the United States.

Representation in the United States is predicated on the clash of interests. All groups are in principle free to express themselves and mobilize supporters. An abundance of research demonstrates that the members of some groups are much better able to press their claims than others—the more affluent, the more educated, the more experienced, and the more socially connected, among others.[28] Yet a key premise of a liberal democracy is that even marginalized groups facing strong headwinds have opportunities to push back. Pushing back might take many forms, from contacting government officials to networking with like-minded individuals, getting involved in protest movements, and participating in election campaigns. The important point is that in a healthy democracy political setbacks are seen, accurately, as only temporary. In theory, as a party or group is targeted by its opponents and suffers a loss, this should spur countermobilization and greater participation by the group's members.

As discussed in greater detail in the next chapter, immigrants in this latest wave of settlement face many impediments to democratic engagement. This was the case even before the transition to the Trump administration, though following this transition the political environment for immigrants became appreciably more hostile. How immigrants have responded to these challenges can tell us a great deal not only about their own trajectories of integration and participation but also about the quality and integrity of democratic politics overall.

We should further stress at the outset that democracy rests on more than the advancement of group interests through mobilization and conflict. In his last major scholarly work, the eminent political theorist E. E. Schattschneider wrote that democracy is "an experiment in the creation of a community. . . . To put it more bluntly, democracy is about the *love* of people."[29] Schattschneider meant that the conflicts that naturally arise through the everyday churn of politics in a free society should be contested and settled within a system based in a shared sense of trust, belonging, and common purpose. Many other writers have expressed similar sentiments.[30] This moral premise is surely being tested at the moment in all quarters of the United States—but perhaps especially in immigrant communities. In chapters 3 and 4, we consider whether immigrants became more cynical and politically alienated following the 2016 election—or not. In chapter 5, we examine patterns of participation, asking whether immigrants are pulling back from political engagement in this more foreboding climate—or engaging even more.

As noted at the outset, much of the analysis that follows draws from original surveys tracking public opinion among Latino immigrants before and after the 2016 elections. (The appendix provides technical information on the administration of these surveys.) We believe that our choice to focus on Latino immigrants in particular is warranted given that debates in the United States about immigration are often, albeit not exclusively, about foreign-born Latinos and migrant flows from Latin America. We certainly recognize, however, that Latin American immigration does not encompass the totality of the immigrant experience in the United States, particularly with a plurality of new migrants now arriving from Asia, and we acknowledge that this focus limits our ability to generalize across the entire diverse population of immigrants in the United States.[31] Nevertheless, in the context of the 2016 elections and its aftermath, leading into Trump's second presidential campaign in 2020, the focus on immigration from Latin America—the administration's bête noir— seems justified.

LIVING CIVIC LIFE ON THE EDGE   2

THE EFFECTS OF DISAPPOINTMENT
AND VULNERABILITY ON IMMIGRANT
POLITICAL INCORPORATION

Losing in politics can hurt. In the aftermath of an electoral defeat, supporters of the losing campaign may feel disappointment and anger and have a sense that the political system has betrayed them. Such feelings may stick with individuals long after an election. One recent study in the academic journal *Emotion* finds, for example, that among Hillary Clinton supporters in 2016, "subjective well-being"—the degree to which they were satisfied with life and feel happy—declined markedly after Clinton's loss relative to their feelings several weeks before the election, when nearly all pundits and voting forecasters were predicting a Clinton victory. When contacted again six months after the election, these measures of subjective well-being among Clinton voters still had not returned to their pre-election baseline.[1] Clearly, many voters take politics quite personally.

This may be especially true for individuals for whom the stakes of an election outcome are unusually high. As discussed in the last chapter, Donald Trump ran for president on an openly anti-immigrant platform, a stance that was 180 degrees different from what Republican Party elders had counseled following the party's loss in 2012. Not only did Trump vow to deport the millions residing without authorization in the United States and end DACA for young undocumented migrants, but he also endorsed ending birthright citizenship, slashing legal immigration by half, and shifting away from the family preferences that have been the central pillar of American immigration policy for the last half-century. Trump's election in 2016 thus signaled the potential for a dramatic change in

U.S. immigration policies that would be likely to have direct negative consequences for many first-generation immigrants to the
United States.

Not surprisingly, media reports in the days after the election
highlighted the manifold concerns that were rippling across immigrant communities. As the banner for one piece on WBUR, a Boston-
area public radio station, put it, "Trump Election Spurs 'Panic' in
Local Immigrant Communities." The report featured commentary
from a local immigration advocate: "We have heard from people that
they are really scared. . . . What should we do? Should we close our
businesses? Should we send our children to school? What's going
to happen with the members of our family?"[2] In the Twin Cities of
Minnesota, the *Star Tribune* reported that "Trump's Victory Triggers
Anxiety Among Minnesota Somalis, Other Immigrants."[3] Most dis-
tressingly, medical professionals across the country reported marked
increases in demand for therapeutic behavioral health services among
immigrants and their families following the election. "It's as though
a volcano erupted. It's been awful," said the director of behavioral
health at the Venice Family Clinic, a major provider of health care to
low-income families in southern California.[4]

Findings from the 2016–2017 Latino Immigrant National Election
Study (LINES) capture these sentiments in the aggregate. In August
and September 2016, 1,800 foreign-born Latinos from across the
United States were randomly selected and interviewed by telephone.
Immediately after the election and continuing through the presidential transition period, which ended on January 20, 2017, as many
of these respondents as possible (N = 576) were interviewed again,
so that changes in attitudes could be gauged. Through the transition
period, a small fresh sample of Latino immigrants were interviewed
as well (N = 260). A third wave of interviews was then conducted
the following summer to assess longer-term changes in opinions
and activities under the Trump administration. At that juncture,
554 of the immigrants from the pre-election period were located
and interviewed, and an additional 500 foreign-born Latinos were
added to the study.[5]

In each survey wave, immigrants shared their opinions on a host
of political topics, many of which are considered in later chapters. Four items in particular speak to a dispirited frame of mind as
the country transitioned from the Obama to the Trump years. First,

Figure 2.1 *"Is the United States Going in the Right Direction, or Are Things on the Wrong Track?": Opinions of Latino Immigrants, 2012–2016*

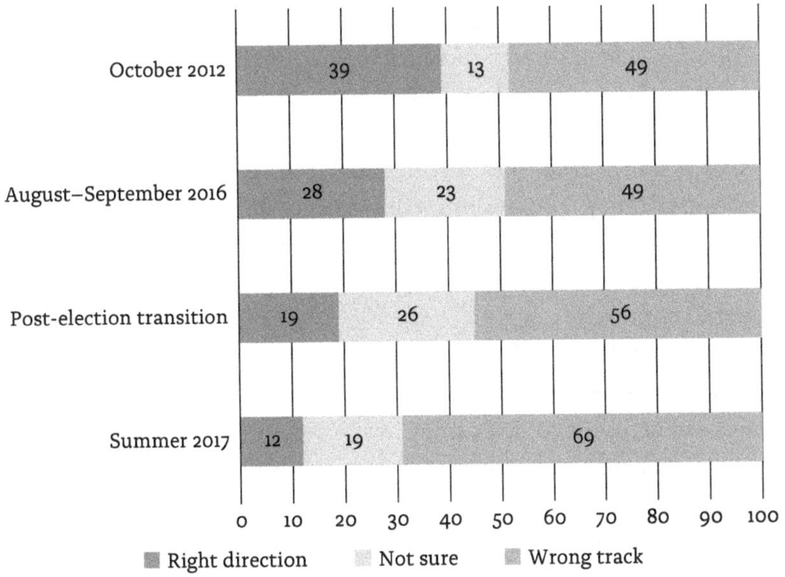

Source: 2012 and 2016–2017 Latino Immigrant National Election Studies.
Note: In this figure and those that follow, percentages may sum to slightly above or slightly below 100 due to rounding.

consider responses to an item that has appeared routinely for decades on public opinion surveys—a question about whether the respondent believes that the country is "generally going in the right direction" or feels that "things have gotten seriously off on the wrong track." This question taps into a general mood about national policymaking and governance. Various polling firms (for example, the CBS News Poll, the USA Today Poll, and the Bloomberg National Poll) have found over the last decade that among the general public, pessimists tend to outnumber optimists by significant margins—by ratios of two-to-one or more in some periods.[6]

In the fall of 2016, the American National Election Study found that among U.S.-born Americans, only 24 percent were pleased with the direction of the country; 75 percent saw the United States as seriously off on the wrong track. Many people in this latter category undoubtedly resonated with the brand of grievance-filled politics featured in the Trump campaign. In contrast, Latino immigrants at this time were significantly more upbeat, as shown in figure 2.1. Only just under half of respondents surveyed in the first wave of the

2016–2017 LINES, in the fall before the 2016 elections, believed that the country was off course. This level of pessimism is largely comparable to that gauged in the fall of 2012, when we conducted a large national survey of foreign-born Latinos using the same sampling procedures as in 2016 (N = 853). One notable difference across these two election cycles, however, was that the 2016 campaign environment featured a higher level of uncertainty. At this time, approximately one out of four LINES respondents was not sure whether or not the United States was moving in a right or worrisome direction—a finding that could well be attributable to the highly unusual set of presidential contenders in 2016 compared to 2012.

Immediately following the 2016 election, pessimism about where the country was going climbed among foreign-born Latinos: nearly six out of ten believed that things were seriously on the wrong track. Pessimism continued to rise once Donald Trump entered the White House. In the summer of 2017, 69 percent of LINES respondents saw the country as off-track, which nearly matched the level of pessimism for U.S.-born Americans before the election. Only 12 percent were satisfied—a far lower level of optimism than what was recorded for the U.S.-born electorate the preceding fall.

In the fall of 2016 and summer of 2017, LINES respondents also reported on their emotional reactions to Donald Trump. Did he spark fear? Anger? Both fear and anger? The breakdown of responses in figure 2.2 tells us that in each period negative emotional reactions were widespread. Only 17 percent of the respondents were neither afraid of nor angry toward Donald Trump both before the election and the following summer. In both survey waves, the most common emotional state was one of both anger and fear. This finding cuts somewhat against news accounts of immigrant reactions to Trump after the election. The dominant theme in much reporting, as illustrated earlier, was the wave of anxiety that hit immigrant communities hard. This news coverage was certainly not inaccurate—our surveys indicate that there was indeed considerable fear in these communities. At the same time, there was also much anger. The emotional mix of immigrants' responses to the elections has implications that are discussed later in this chapter.

Two additional items, both asked in the second and third survey waves, addressed more personal concerns. How worried was the

Figure 2.2 *Emotional Reactions of Latino Immigrants to Donald Trump, 2016–2017*

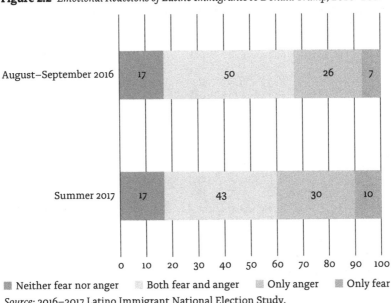

August–September 2016: 17, 50, 26, 7

Summer 2017: 17, 43, 30, 10

■ Neither fear nor anger   ■ Both fear and anger   ■ Only anger   ■ Only fear

Source: 2016–2017 Latino Immigrant National Election Study.
Note: In each survey wave, immigrants were asked if they felt anger toward Donald Trump, and then they were asked if they felt afraid of him. Responses were combined to make these scales.

respondent that a close friend or family member might be deported? And how worried was he or she about the financial situation of his or her family? Response categories ranged from "not at all" to "extremely" worried. In figures 2.3 and 2.4, we see consistently high levels of anxiety. With Donald Trump as the president-elect and then later as president, only a small fraction of the LINES sample (20 and 17 percent, respectively) voiced no concerns about the possible deportation of friends or family members. At the opposite end of the continuum, greater numbers reported being extremely anxious. We do not have pre-election data to benchmark these findings. But surveys conducted by the Pew Hispanic Center in the fall of 2013 and summer of 2018 suggest an appreciable uptick in deportation worries under Trump. Both Pew polls included a question that was comparable to the LINES item: "Regardless of your own immigration or citizenship status, how much, if at all, do you worry that you, a family member, or a close friend could be deported? Would you say that you worry a lot (coded 4), some (3), not much (2), or not at all (1)?"

Figure 2.3 *"How Worried Are You That a Close Friend or Family Member May Be Deported?": Changes in Latino Immigrants' Concern from November 2016 to Summer 2017*

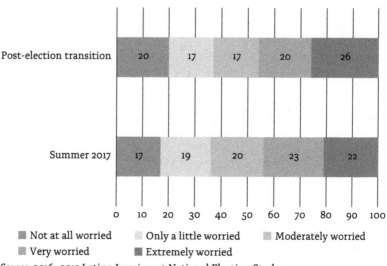

Not at all worried   Only a little worried   Moderately worried
Very worried   Extremely worried

Source: 2016–2017 Latino Immigrant National Election Study.

Figure 2.4 *"How Worried Are You About the Current Financial Situation for You and Your Family?": Changes in Latino Immigrants' Concern from November 2016 to Summer 2017*

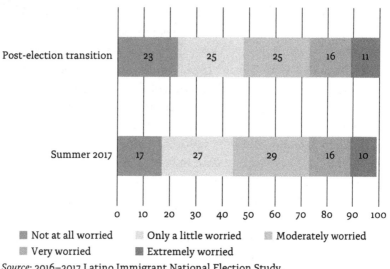

Not at all worried   Only a little worried   Moderately worried
Very worried   Extremely worried

Source: 2016–2017 Latino Immigrant National Election Study.

Among the foreign-born Latinos in these surveys, 59 percent reported worrying "a lot" or "some" in 2013; in 2018, this percentage stood at 67 percent.[7]

Latino immigrants were also concerned about their financial well-being and that of their families in the aftermath of the 2016 election. During the Trump transition period and then six months later, over half of the LINES respondents were at least moderately concerned about finances. Although the number of immigrants reporting no concerns at all dipped slightly over time, the average level of anxiety about finances did not change significantly in the period before the election to the period after it ($p = .23$).

It is worth noting that worries about the deportation of friends or family and concerns about personal finances overlapped to a modest extent in both the post-election transition period and the summer of 2017. This might lead to the conclusion that some people are simply worriers, exhibiting a generalized anxiety across a number of dimensions. These correlations, however, while statistically significant, are not so large as to suggest that a summary "personal worry profile" could be gauged for respondents.[8] This being the case, we might expect to observe distinctive effects of such anxieties—and of the two other indicators of civic stress—on immigrant political incorporation.

Variations in Civic Stress During the First Year of the Trump Administration

Figures 2.1 to 2.4 highlight how widespread pessimism, fear, and anger were within the Latino immigrant community following the 2016 election. It was a rare immigrant in the first year of the Trump administration who expressed no such negative feelings.[9] To map the contours of civic stresses more fully, we next consider how responses to these items varied by citizenship status, time spent in the United States, respondents' state of residence, and whether or not they had emigrated from Mexico.

Immigrants who are naturalized U.S. citizens have many more rights and opportunities than noncitizens. The right to vote in federal elections, granted only to citizens, certainly stands out in principle as the most significant. But citizenship bestows a wide array of more tangible benefits as well. It is generally easier for naturalized immigrants to utilize government services in areas like health care, education, and unemployment relief. Compared to noncitizens, citizens also have access to a much broader range of employers, and that translates into more lucrative salaries.[10] To illustrate, among the naturalized Latino citizens in the 2016 LINES study, only one-quarter reported a modest family income below $25,000. For green card holders (legal permanent residents), this figure rose to 38 percent, and it was still higher—44 percent— for noncitizen respondents who did not have a green card.[11] Naturalized citizens also face little risk of deportation and are able to move about much more freely in their day-to-day activities. In short, the harsh anti-immigrant policies and rhetoric emanating from the White House are liable to be significantly less threatening to foreign-born Latinos who are U.S. citizens. Consequently, we might expect to see somewhat lower levels of civic stress among respondents with citizenship rights during the first year of the Trump administration.

The number of years an immigrant has lived in the United States could also influence levels of civic stress. Over time, immigrants tend to put down roots in a local community—their involvement in volunteer organizations and civic activities increases, their interpersonal social networks become denser and more diverse, and they achieve a higher socioeconomic status.[12] To be sure, there is not an exact functional relationship between length of residence in the United States and communal integration. Trajectories of inclusion naturally vary. Yet in general, "integration increases over time, with immigrants becoming more like the native-born with more time in the country."[13] In the 2016–2017 LINES data set, there was substantial variation in time spent in the United States. The average length of stay was twenty-three years, a substantial investment of time. One-quarter of the sample, however, reported having lived in the country less than fifteen years; at the other end of this range, one-quarter had resided in the United States for more than thirty-one years. As with immigrants who have become naturalized citizens, foreign-born Latinos with more experience living in the country could feel less vulnerable to anti-immigrant policies and pressures relative to newcomers. Their feelings of civic stress under Trump may consequently be lower.

LINES respondents who resided in states that are more welcoming toward immigrants may also have exhibited less civic stress. Over the last twenty years, efforts within the U.S. Congress to cobble together comprehensive immigration policy reform have failed owing to gridlock over what such reform should entail. Prioritizing border security? Establishing a pathway to citizenship for immigrants without papers? Issuing work visas with greater administrative flexibility? Expanding multicultural social services? Detaining and deporting as many undocumented immigrants as possible? Absent a policy consensus at the federal level, lawmakers in state capitals have taken it upon themselves to enact statutes that affect immigrants in a multitude of ways—some for the better, some for the worse.

In a recent study of tensions between state and federal authorities over immigration, Gary Reich provides an inventory of pro- and anti-immigrant measures within the states that were in force as of 2017.[14] His listing of welcoming statutes includes: in-state tuition for undocumented students; state financial aid for undocumented students; issuance of driver's licenses to immigrants who are undocumented; programs to provide health care to unauthorized immigrants; Medicaid coverage for lawfully residing immigrants without a five-year wait; and state coverage for lawfully residing immigrant children without a five-year wait. Thirty-four states had one or more of these policies on the books in the first year of the Trump administration. On the other hand, twenty-five states had adopted one or more of the following restrictive policies toward immigrants: mandatory immigration checks when detained and/or compliance with Immigration and Customs Enforcement (ICE) detainer requests; a ban on in-state tuition for undocumented students; no immigrant health care spending beyond federally mandated minimums; required use of E-Verify for most public-sector hires; and required use of E-Verify for private-sector hires.[15]

Figure 2.5 displays the dramatic variations in state-level policies toward immigrants. Here we have calculated a differential score that reflects the political disposition of a state—the number of accommodating statutes minus the number of restrictive statutes. Since five anti-immigrant and six pro-immigrant measures are tallied, this score ranges from –5 to +6. At the positive end of this continuum, California, Illinois, and Washington stand out as particularly friendly

Figure 2.5 *Differences in Immigration Policies in Twenty-Five States, from Most Accommodating to Most Restrictive, 2017*

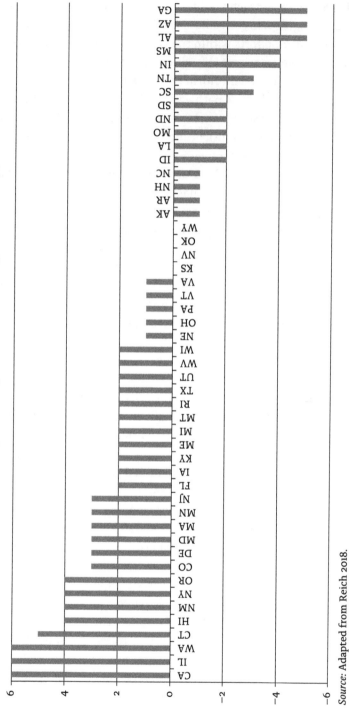

Source: Adapted from Reich 2018.

Note: See main text for examples of accommodating policies and restrictive policies.

toward immigrants, while Alabama, Arizona, and Georgia are the most restrictive. Within the LINES data set, relatively few respondents lived in these latter states. But there is still considerable variability in the political climates to which survey participants were exposed. Approximately one-third of respondents were California residents. Another one-third of the sample lived in either Florida or Texas, states that were relatively more neutral in their policy dispositions toward immigrants. Both of these states provide in-state tuition to undocumented students and timely Medicaid coverage for lawfully residing immigrants, among other supportive measures. But both also require the use of E-Verify for public-sector hiring, and Texas mandates compliance with ICE detainer requests. Overall, the average score across respondents on the −5 to +6 state policy scale is slightly over 3.0, suggesting that the typical immigrant in the data set lived in a state that was just moderately welcoming.

These differences in state-level policies—often labeled "immigration federalism"—spring from several factors. Karthick Ramakrishnan and Pratheepan Gulasekaram note that partisan contexts matter a great deal. Republican-leaning states tend to pass more restrictive immigration legislation, though the needs of agricultural interests for immigrant labor often check this impulse.[16] James Monogan suggests that state wealth is also a factor; in poorer states, legislators may find it more difficult to persuade the native-born population that extending benefits to immigrants is appropriate.[17] On the other hand, more prosperous states that lean Democratic and have a long tradition of incorporating earlier waves of migrants tend to enact statutes that are more accommodating toward immigrants. This describes California quite well.

In states where immigrants are afforded greater benefits and opportunities, the political transition to the Trump era may have been less unsettling. When assessing the turn that the country had taken, the potential threats from the White House, and the well-being of family and friends, immigrants in states like California, Illinois, and Washington may have taken solace in the robust layers of protection and support provided by state lawmakers. Immigrants living in less welcoming states, feeling more at risk, may have voiced greater pessimism, anxiety, and anger.

We further consider whether immigrants from Mexico were especially prone to express concerns about where the country was heading, the well-being of family and friends, and the president himself in the post-2016 environment. Just over six out of ten LINES respondents were Mexican-origin, a proportion in keeping with current census figures. As detailed in the previous introductory chapter, Trump launched his presidential campaign in mid-2015 with a string of insults directed against Mexicans. The candidate charged that, among other things, Mexican migrants engaged in rampant drug trafficking and were prone to committing violent crimes. Fact-checkers found such statements easy to debunk.[18] There is no evidence that Mexican-born immigrants are involved in more criminal activities than native-born Americans, and indeed there is evidence to the contrary. Yet Trump's rhetoric at this defining moment in his campaign, along with his push to put up a wall to separate Mexico and the United States, might have made Mexican immigrants feel particularly stigmatized, and in turn raised their levels of civic stress.[19]

Turning to the LINES survey findings, are citizenship status, length of residence in the United States, state-level policy climates, and emigration from Mexico rather than another Latin American country in fact related to the four civic stress items? We observe some suggestive patterns, which are presented in figures 2.6 to 2.9. On the whole, however, immigrants who would presumably be less vulnerable to the anti-immigrant agenda of the new administration still expressed about as much disappointment, anger, and fear as the more vulnerable.

We focus first on the "wrong track"/"right direction" item. Figure 2.6 shows fluctuations across subgroups in the belief that the United States was heading in the wrong direction in the summer of 2017. For the full LINES sample, 69 percent of respondents were pessimistic. As expected, immigrants who were not citizens and did not hold a green card were even more pessimistic. However, the margin rose only to 73 percent for these respondents, as opposed to 70 percent for green card recipients and 66 percent for naturalized citizens. These differences are not statistically significant. Nor did the number of years an immigrant had lived in the United States shape attitudes about the direction of the country, contrary to expectations. The correlation between length of stay in the country and the "wrong track"/"right direction" item is essentially

Figure 2.6 *Subsample Variations in the Belief That the United States Is on the Wrong Track, Summer 2017*

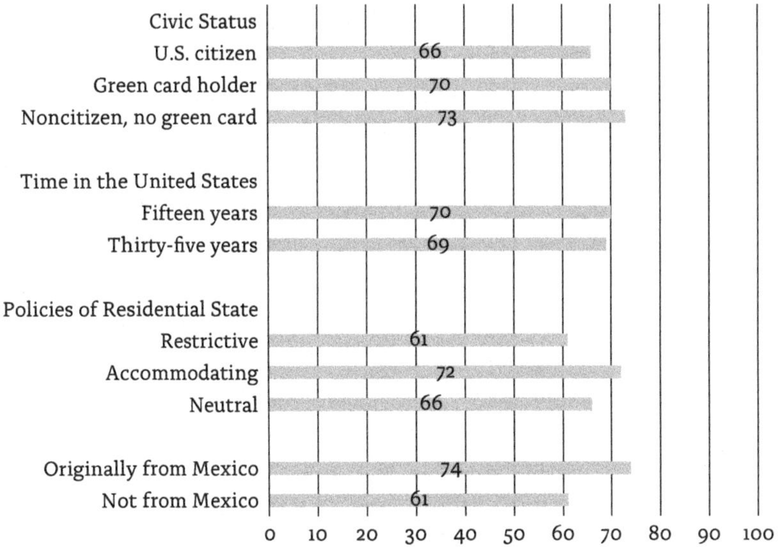

Source: 2016–2017 Latino Immigrant National Election Study.

Note: Civic status, time in the United States, and state policy orientations were not significantly related to beliefs about the direction of the country; Mexicans were significantly more pessimistic compared to immigrants from other countries. The relationships between civic status, Mexican origin, and evaluations of where the United States was heading were assessed through cross-tabulation. Since time spent in the United States and state-level policy dispositions were coded on a continuum, ordinal logistic regression models were fit to gauge the impact of these variables on pessimism about the direction of the country. The percentages for respondents who had lived in the United States for fifteen or thirty-five years and for respondents who resided in a restrictive, accommodating, or neutral state are predicted values derived from these regressions. For illustrative purposes, a "restrictive" state is coded as –5, the lowest point on the policy scale shown in figure 2.5; an "accommodating" state was scored as +6, the highest value of the scale; and a "neutral" state was coded as 0 on this scale.

zero. We illustrate this by presenting the levels of pessimism for two hypothetical Latino immigrants—one who had lived in the United States for fifteen years and another who had lived here for thirty-five years. In these cases, the percentages—70 versus 69 percent—are essentially indistinguishable.[20]

Looking to the lower part of figure 2.6, we see that immigrants who lived in a more welcoming state were actually somewhat more likely to be pessimistic about where the United States was heading compared to those living in a restrictive or neutral state. This too cuts against expectations; we had posited that residence in an immigrant-friendly state would encourage optimism. However, these differences in percentages—61, 72, and 66 percent—are not statistically different from one another.[21] For purposes of illustration, a "welcoming" state is defined here by a score of +6 on the policy scale shown in figure 2.5, the highest possible value. A "restrictive" state is one that scored –5, the lowest scale value, and a neutral state is coded as 0. The fact that state policy climates had little to do with pessimistic feelings tells us that the benefits and support extended to immigrants in states like California, Illinois, and Washington—provisions that improve the quality of life for a great many of the foreign-born and their families—were not reassuring to LINES respondents as they considered the overall direction of the country.

In the lower part of this figure we see that Mexicans tended to be more pessimistic than other immigrants. The difference of thirteen points (74 versus 61 percent) is statistically significant, and it comports with expectations. Just the same, it is appropriate to conclude, based on these findings and the others presented here, that disappointment over the direction of the country extended far and wide across the entire Latino immigrant population.

The percentages in figure 2.7 further show that in the summer of 2017 substantial numbers of respondents felt afraid of or angry toward President Trump regardless of their citizenship status, length of time spent in the United States, state of residence, and whether or not they had emigrated from Mexico. Latino immigrants who were not naturalized citizens and lacked a green card were somewhat more likely to express fear and anger: the margin for this combination was 49 percent, as opposed to 39 percent for naturalized citizens. But this difference is not statistically significant. Along similar lines, respondents who had lived in the United States for thirty-five years were less prone to negative emotional reactions in comparison to immigrants with only fifteen years of residency in the country, though this difference in percentages is also insignificant. Furthermore, there is no noteworthy variation in fear or anger based on state of residence. Immigrants in more welcoming states were as perturbed as those in more restrictive states. Nor were Mexicans significantly

Figure 2.7 *Subsample Variations in Negative Emotional Reactions to Donald Trump, Summer 2017*

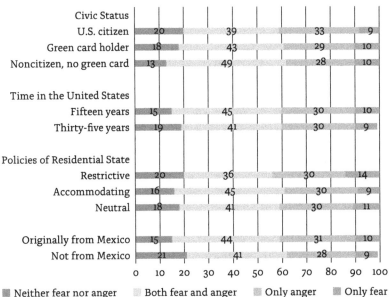

Neither fear nor anger　　Both fear and anger　　Only anger　　Only fear

Source: 2016–2017 Latino Immigrant National Election Study.

Note: Civic status, time in the United States, policy orientation of the residential state toward immigrants, and being from Mexico were not significantly related to emotional reactions to President Trump. The relationships between civic status and emotional reactions were assessed through cross-tabulation. The effects of time spent in the United States and state-level policy dispositions were assessed through multinomial logistic regression.

more inclined than immigrants from other Latin American countries to be anxious or angry about Trump. These findings match those in the preceding figure. When considering the direction that the country had taken after the 2016 election and the tone of leadership coming from the White House, Latino immigrants were generally of one mind: relatively few were at ease.

Figures 2.8 and 2.9 show variations across subgroups in respondents' worries about the possible deportation of friends or family members and about family finances. For both items, noncitizens without a green card expressed more pronounced anxiety compared to legal permanent residents and naturalized citizens. The difference in probabilities of worrying about deportation is statistically

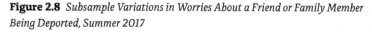

Figure 2.8 *Subsample Variations in Worries About a Friend or Family Member Being Deported, Summer 2017*

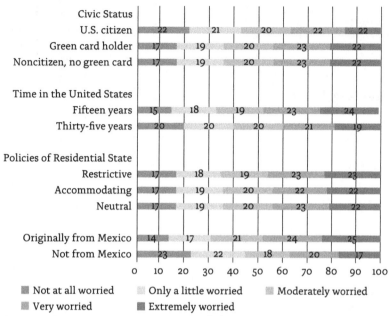

Source: 2016–2017 Latino Immigrant National Election Study.

Note: Civic status, time spent in the United States, and being from Mexico were significantly related to deportation worries. The relationships between civic status, Mexican origin, and deportation concerns were assessed through cross-tabulation. The effects of time spent in the United States and state-level policy dispositions were assessed through ordinal logistic regression.

significant. This is not to say, however, that naturalized immigrants were free from worry. Far from it—approximately eight out of ten citizens voiced some degree of concern about deportations and finances.

In a comparable vein, the number of years a survey respondent had lived in the United States correlates with both kinds of worries, with longer-term residents being less concerned. In the case of deportations, 20 percent of immigrants who had lived in the country for thirty-five years are predicted through our statistical analysis not to have been worried at all. For respondents who had been in the United States only fifteen years, this decreased to 15 percent, a statistically significant decline but still a fairly slight drop. This difference in percentages is similar to what is observed for worries

Figure 2.9 *Subsample Variations in Worries About Family Finances, Summer 2017*

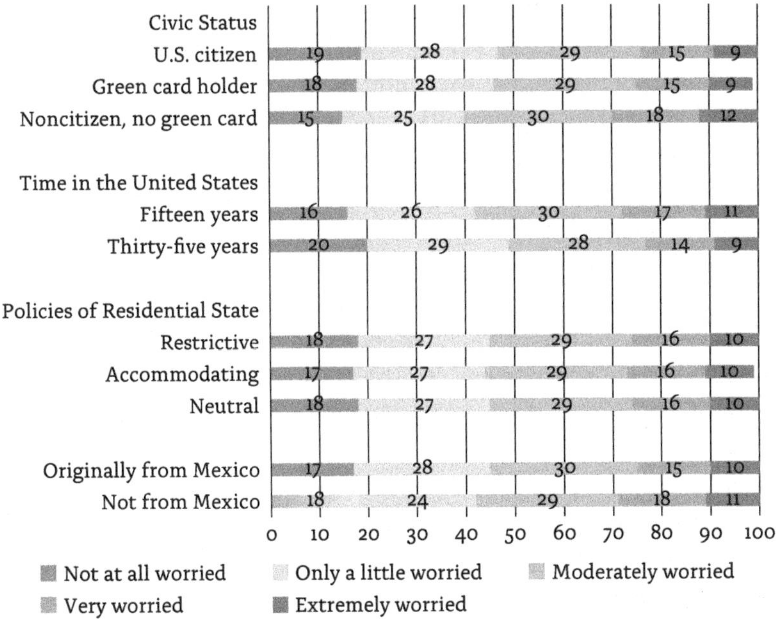

Source: 2016–2017 Latino Immigrant National Election Study.

Note: Time spent in the United States was significantly related to financial worries. The relationships between civic status, Mexican origin, and financial concerns were assessed through cross-tabulation. The effects of time spent in the United States and state-level policy dispositions were assessed through ordinal logistic regression.

about family finances. Immigrants with more time in the United States were somewhat less inclined to express concerns. But the variation here is slight. As noted in figure 2.9, 20 percent of LINES respondents who had lived in the country for thirty-five years voiced no worries about finances, as opposed to 16 percent among those who had been here only fifteen years. At the other end of the scale, approximately one out of ten were extremely worried about finances, regardless of whether they had spent fifteen or thirty-five years in the country.

In the lower parts of figures 2.8 and 2.9, we see that state-level policy dispositions toward immigrants had little to do with how worried respondents were about deportations or finances. These nonfindings are at odds with our earlier expectations. States like California, Washington, Illinois, and the others on the more "welcoming" end of the scale in figure 2.5 offer a number of important benefits and protections to immigrants. Federal agents seeking to detain and deport an immigrant in these states would have to overcome more administrative hurdles than in, say, Georgia. There are also more work opportunities and a more generous social safety net for immigrants in these welcoming states. Objectively, then, it would be reasonable for immigrants in these states to feel more at ease in comparison to respondents living in states where more restrictive policies are on the books.

Yet feelings are, of course, subjective. The anti-immigrant posture of the White House under Trump was exceedingly expansive in its scope. As discussed earlier, the president not only called for stepped-up deportations of undocumented immigrants but also sought to limit the number of green cards being issued. And President Trump frequently disparaged the entire Latino immigrant community, among other immigrant nationality groups, even if he singled out Mexicans when launching his political campaign. These sentiments came across most bluntly in a meeting with lawmakers in January 2018, when Trump held up Norwegians as ideal immigrants while using foul, derogatory language to describe migrant-sending countries in the developing world.[22] It is thus understandable that in the Trump era, foreign-born Latinos across the board—citizens and noncitizens, longer-term and shorter-term residents, and the residents of both welcoming and unwelcoming states—would tend to see themselves as coequally under attack and in precarious positions.[23] In the lower part of figures 2.8 and 2.9, we find that Mexicans were slightly more likely to be worried about deportations and finances: the difference between the Mexican-born and other nationality groups was statistically significant when respondents expressed concerns about possible deportations. The data clearly indicate, however, that the vast majority of immigrants, Mexicans and all others, felt at risk in the first year of the Trump administration.

Implications for Democratic Inclusion

How might these widespread feelings of disappointment, anger, and fear have affected trajectories of Latino immigrant inclusion into American democracy? In the chapters that follow, we consider the potentially corrosive implications of civic stress through a close examination of three essential pillars of democratic inclusivity:

1. *Faith in the legitimacy of American governing authorities:* Faith in political authority should not be unquestioning or blind. When officials make mistakes, become embroiled in scandals, or otherwise act contrary to citizens' interests, it is reasonable to question whether representative institutions on the whole are performing adequately. Yet it has long been recognized that effective policymaking and accountability in a democracy depend on broad acceptance of government institutions. In one highly influential work published in 1965, David Easton distinguished between an individual's "specific" support for particular political programs and more "diffuse" support for the system on the whole. "Where such [diffuse] support threatens to fall below a minimal level, regardless of the cause, the system must either provide mechanisms to revise the flagging support or its days will be numbered."[24] Along similar lines, Gabriel Almond and Sidney Verba's 1963 analysis in *The Civic Culture* of five very different democracies sees "system affect" (that is, "generalized attitudes towards the system as a whole") as a key prerequisite for resilient democratic representation.[25] Any consideration of immigrant political incorporation should therefore take into account dispositions toward national political institutions in the United States, how these attitudes compare to those of the native-born, and how these dispositions may change for those who feel pessimistic about the direction of the country, angry at the head of state, or personally vulnerable.

2. *Interpersonal trust and an affective attachment to the country:* Perhaps more important than "diffuse support" and "system affect" for stable and sound democratic governance is a shared sense of interpersonal trust among people and an abiding affection for the country and its ideals. Trust among the diverse members of a democratic society promotes tolerance for opposing viewpoints. In democracies where there is widespread interpersonal trust, politics is also less of a zero-sum game, and compromises over policy become more feasible.[26] So too patriotic attitudes toward one's country—the positive feelings engendered when seeing the flag fly, for instance—can promote social solidarity and reinforce

empathetic emotional connections among compatriots.[27] When assessing the trajectory of immigrant incorporation into American democracy and society, it is therefore important to consider the dynamics of interpersonal trust and feelings about the United States.

3. *Political involvement:* Clearly, in thinking about democratic incorporation, actual participation in politics is essential to track as well. Involvement is, after all, the key expression of political voice in a democracy. Most immigrants in the United States today are not naturalized citizens and therefore cannot vote in federal elections.[28] But all residents, citizens and non-citizens alike, are free to engage in politics in any number of other ways—attending meetings on public issues within one's local community, contacting government officials, attending campaign events, or, when the times call for it, taking to the streets in marches and protest demonstrations. Of course, there is no guaranteeing that an expression of political voice will result in meaningful representation. Officials may never hear such voices, or they may simply dismiss them out of hand. However, individuals who do not express themselves at all for whatever reasons are clearly at a disadvantage. Consequently, any assessment of immigrant incorporation into American democracy must take a close look at political participation and the forces that prompt or impede it.

How would the kinds of disappointments and negative emotions documented in figures 2.1 to 2.4 affect these different facets of democratic incorporation? Psychologists examining the ways in which emotions guide decisions and shape attitudes generally agree that anger is a mobilizing or "approach" emotion. That is, angry people are prone to take action, sometimes ignoring risks at their great peril. Anyone who has encountered an angry driver on the road or even an angry fan at a sports event can attest to these effects. In politics, anger prompts participation in a wide array of activities—voting, running for office, grassroots organizing, protesting, and, in extreme cases, revolutionary behavior to topple a government.[29]

A belief that an injustice has occurred tends to arouse feelings of anger—a sense of righteous indignation or betrayal. It is thus not surprising that the LINES survey found so much anger among Latino immigrants directed toward Donald Trump. Indeed, it would have been odd if Trump's statements and actions both as a candidate for office and as president had not provoked a good amount of righteous indignation within this population. Anger at Donald Trump could cast a shadow over U.S. governing institutions—and perhaps, more alarmingly, over the American public at large, which elected Trump in the first place. If anger toward the president has such expansive effects, the trajectory of immigrant incorporation into American democracy could well be derailed. Chapters 3 and 4 consider these themes. We further expect that such feelings would lead many immigrants to take action, especially in protest marches and street demonstrations, the most accessible setting for many to express their dissatisfaction. We examine these dynamics in chapter 5.

There is a general consensus among researchers about the potential ramifications of anger in politics, but the effects of fear and pessimism are more difficult to predict in any given context. Perceptions of threat and anxiety may motivate people in many instances to seek safety while becoming more watchful within their immediate environment.[30] One implication of this for foreign-born Latinos is that feelings of being under siege or apprehension about the direction of the country could lead to suspicions about political authorities and withdrawal from civic life.

It is even possible that misgivings and fears regarding the direction of the country or the well-being of family and friends could cause immigrants to reconsider their decision to live in the United States. It is common during political campaigns for American voters to exclaim that "if [he/she] wins, I'm moving to Canada!" There is little evidence to suggest that political disappointments experienced by the general public actually prompt such emigration.[31] Yet for the vast majority of immigrants in the United States—all except refugees and asylum-seekers—an "exit option" from the country under duress could be a real option. Needless to say, the long-term incorporation of Latino immigrants into American democracy would be severely undermined if pessimism and anxieties about politics prompted such suspicion and withdrawal.

These implications notwithstanding, Erdem Aytac and Susan Stokes make the point in their recent comparative analysis of voting turnout and protest activism that anxieties about political conditions can lead people to be not only more cautious and risk-averse but also more ready for action. Those "who become fearful can also be aroused to act to forestall outcomes that frighten them."[32] And in practice, fear and anger often become intermingled. Situations that cause one to become afraid often also bring out anger. This is very much evident in figure 2.2, where the modal reaction to Donald Trump among LINES respondents was both emotions.

Investigations to date in the scholarly literature on "emotions and politics" do not point to any clear expectations regarding the joint impact of anger and fear on political attitudes and activities. If fears prompt "avoidance" of risks and stressors rather than "approach," as many authors posit, it is possible that immigrants who felt both afraid of and angry toward Donald Trump would not be as assertive as respondents who expressed only anger. That is, we may observe a kind of emotional "cross-pressuring," where one negative emotional state checks the other.

On the other hand, a long-standing tradition in psychological research suggests that distinctive negative emotions such as fearfulness, distress, hostility, and scornfulness are sufficiently clustered that they influence an individual's attitudes and choices in broadly similar ways.[33] If this is the case for LINES respondents, feeling both angry and afraid about Trump could have an outsized impact on political attitudes and participation relative to feeling only angry or only afraid. Whatever the implications of negative emotions for immigrant incorporation into American democracy, this latter perspective would lead us to expect especially strong effects when anger over Trump coincides with fear.

The items in figures 2.1 to 2.4 cover a very wide range of concerns—concerns about a powerful public figure who is antagonistic toward immigrants, misgivings about where the country on the whole is heading, and worries about the well-being of those within one's immediate personal network. We anticipate that all of these items could shape not only attitudes toward U.S. governing institutions but also more general attitudes toward the American public. Such distress may prompt political participation as well. As researchers, we had no strong expectations in designing this study about the relative impact of each item on political attitudes and behavior.

It is possible, however, that anxieties regarding the financial well-being of one's family would carry less weight vis-à-vis the other concerns. Worries about finances are no doubt profoundly salient for immigrants, as they would be for anyone else. Yet within the wider American electorate, people who find themselves in difficult financial straits tend not to attribute their situation to political factors. To account for their personal financial difficulties, they might cite bad luck, unemployment caused by poor management at the workplace, or a lack of proper training for an advanced position within a firm—among other such factors. Such explanations direct attention away from more political considerations. "Under ordinary circumstances," write Donald Kinder and Roderick Kiewiet, "voters evidently do not make connections between their own personal economic experiences—however vivid, immediate and otherwise significant—and their political attitudes and preferences."[34]

The strong streak of individualism deeply embedded in U.S. political culture keeps many Americans from blaming governing institutions or society in general for their financial woes.[35] It might also be challenging for individuals to connect the actions taken by government policymakers to one's immediate financial situation; it may be far from obvious how, say, corporate tax rates, international trade policies, or governmental infrastructure projects affect one's own pocketbook.[36] If this holds for foreign-born Latinos, worries about personal financial well-being may influence political attitudes and activities somewhat less compared to concerns about the deportation of family members and friends, the overall direction that the country is moving in, and Donald Trump himself. These three concerns are directly tied to evaluations of political actors and government policies. As such, they may be more relevant as immigrants consider the legitimacy of representative institutions in the United States, whether Americans on the whole are trustworthy, and whether or not they should take part in politics.

The three chapters that follow sort out the various implications of Latino immigrants' worries, disappointments, and anger in response to the 2016 elections for their incorporation into American democracy.

THE EFFECT OF CIVIC STRESS ON FAITH IN AMERICAN GOVERNMENT

3

LESS TINT IN THE ROSE-COLORED GLASSES?

How often can Americans trust government officials in Washington, D.C., to do the right thing? Is the government actually run for the benefit of all, or do only a few big interests control it? How widespread is corruption and malfeasance in our political institutions?

At any gathering of friends or family in the United States, questions such as these easily come up when conversation turns to politics. Many people may find it hard to discuss the intricacies of policies and legal regulations, and the workings of different government offices can seem truly mysterious to outsiders. Yet most Americans have no problem commenting—some quite vociferously—on the trustworthiness of politicians and speculating about whether policymakers are in the pocket of "special interests." We know that individuals readily call to mind judgments about the integrity of governing institutions because academic researchers have been polling on this subject from the dawning of scientific survey sampling in the 1930s. These evaluations are regularly tracked because in a democracy the level of people's faith in elected officials bears directly on the health and well-being of the political system. "Public trust," writes the political theorist Mark Warren, "is the *sine qua non* of a democracy's capacities to get things done."[1]

When faith in political authorities rather than cynicism toward them is widespread, members of society are more inclined to comply with government policies and follow the law, even if those policies and laws impose significant costs.[2] Politics becomes less of a zero-sum competition, election campaigns are less divisive, and officials have more latitude to bargain and compromise. Moreover, when careers in politics are seen as prestigious and honorable, the candidates who throw their hat into the ring to seek high office in the first place may be more public-spirited, experienced, and talented.[3] In their classic 1963 comparative study of political culture and democratic performance in West Germany, Italy, Mexico, Great Britain, and the United States, Gabriel Almond and Sidney Verba attribute the relative stability and inclusiveness of representative institutions in the United States to the public's enduring reservoir of political trust.[4] Writing more recently and focusing on fledgling democracies in the developing world, Pippa Norris takes up this point, arguing that in these countries trust in government is a necessary precondition for the effective consolidation of democracy.[5] Economic crises and external shocks are far easier to weather when the public has confidence in elected officials.

Of course, citizens' faith in their government should not be blind and unquestioning; such faith would be just as corrosive for democratic politics as no faith at all. The U.S. Constitution is premised on a healthy skepticism about the kinds of people who are driven to obtain political power. James Madison, the chief architect of the Constitution, and the other framers had no illusions about the potential corruptibility and unreliability of government leaders. In his incisive *Federalist 10*, Madison cautioned strongly against placing unconditional faith in the government. To be sure, "enlightened statesmen" could help sustain and advance a free society. But, as Madison famously argued in this essay, "enlightened statesmen will not always be at the helm." More likely is the possibility that self-interested leaders will "vex and oppress each other" as they contend "for pre-eminence and power."[6]

To counteract these tendencies, American political institutions are set up so that power is dispersed and checked, and the ambitions of self-interested leaders are directed toward satisfying the demands of the public, at least in theory. This is the crux of liberal democracy. Authority to make policies is temporarily delegated to government officials with the expectation that they are answerable to those affected by these policies. If members of the public are too deferential toward those in power—if we put on rose-colored glasses and always assume the best about lawmakers and the institutions within which they operate—representative democracy will not work. When governmental leaders fail us or threaten our interests and well-being, it is reasonable to question whether the system on the whole has become less trustworthy and is morally unsound. Individuals with a healthy skepticism about officials, à la Madison, are mindful of the possibility of such failings. Losing a certain amount of faith in governing institutions when warranted is critical to accountability and a necessary step toward reform.[7]

There is little doubt that scandals, fiascos, and mismanagement within government lead voters to doubt the reliability and integrity of officials. Case in point: in the 1958 American National Election Study, three out of four respondents stated that they trusted the government in Washington, D.C., to do the "right thing" all or most of the time, as opposed to only some of the time—a remarkably positive appraisal. Eighteen years later, this level of trust (as measured in the 1976 ANES) had dropped by more than half, to 34 percent. This decline in perceived trustworthiness came about amid deep concerns about the direction of the country and its foreign policy, reports of wrongdoing in high places, the resignations of a president and vice president to avoid impeachment hearings, assassinations of several prominent political figures, and social protests in all parts of the country. In such a volatile and disconcerting environment, it would have been eminently sensible to question the legitimacy of national policymaking institutions. For their part, congressional leaders took note of the rising cynicism and attempted to restore faith in representative bodies through a number of reforms to limit the influence of major donors in political campaigns, make government proceedings more transparent, and codify ethical standards for officials, among other measures.

Research on political trust in the years since the 1970s has pointed to what may be a chronically high degree of suspiciousness about government officials, even when the national economy is performing relatively well and there is little civil unrest. Over the last decade, for example, fewer than one out of three Americans have expressed trust in government authorities most or all of the time.[8] Such a lack of support arguably goes beyond the "healthy skepticism" that is a necessary part of governance in any democracy. Several explanations have been offered to account for this seemingly persistent knee-jerk cynicism. Some commentators highlight the impact of rising economic inequality, which undercuts the premise that government serves the interests of all people fairly. Others link declining political trust in the United States to partisan polarization. As the major parties stake out more distinct or extreme positions, partisan individuals may automatically assume the worst about officials in the opposing camp. Still others posit that fragmentation within the news media environment these days contributes to declining faith in political institutions; to attract viewers, the criticism goes, an inordinate amount of attention is paid to scandals and policymaking mishaps. Whatever the causes, widespread disillusionment with government today might well put representative institutions on a shakier foundation.[9]

In this chapter, we consider whether the many civic stresses discussed earlier among foreign-born Latinos following the 2016 elections brought about a loss of faith in American governing institutions, and if so, whether this decline suggests a level of disillusionment that parallels what has been observed for the public at large. Recall that these stress items touch on a wide range of concerns: pessimism about where the country is headed; worries that a close friend or family member will be deported; anxieties about the financial well-being of one's family; and negative emotional reactions to Donald Trump (fear and/or anger). Previous research on the dynamics of political trust and legitimacy would lead us to expect that feelings such as these have major effects.

Fears about deportation, finances, and Trump might be particularly consequential in comparison to anger, in that anxieties are thought to trigger heightened surveillance of the immediate environment, with an eye on the lookout for threats. Immigrants who are worried about the future might understandably grow more risk-averse when evaluating government officials, trusting them less in principle and doubting whether they are acting to further the larger interests of society with moral integrity. On its own, anger may not stoke the same level of guardedness and surveillance.[10] But on the whole, each of the civic stress items could in theory diminish systemic legitimacy.

Before moving to the findings, two qualifications should be placed on this expectation. First, the design of the LINES panel survey allows us to gauge the impact of pessimism, worry, and anger in two very different political climates: the presidential transition months from early November 2016 to late January 2017—a period when Barack Obama remained in the White House—and the middle of the first year of the Trump administration. From one survey period to the next, the general posture of the federal government toward immigration and multiculturalism changed dramatically as Trump took a far harder line against immigration than Obama (and indeed, all other presidents in the postwar era) had taken.

As discussed in chapter 2, Latino immigrants during the presidential transition period voiced considerable worry about where the country was headed, whether someone close to them was in danger of deportation, and whether their families would remain economically solvent. This was in addition to the substantial amount of fear and anger that Donald Trump himself aroused as a presidential candidate before the election. These feelings were no doubt highly salient for respondents. Yet during the transition, with Barack Obama still serving as president, negative feelings toward Trump would probably not have led to a loss of faith in U.S. governing institutions. Nor might the other civic stress items have had as much of an impact at this juncture, since the federal government under Obama's leadership would probably not have been viewed as the driving force behind such stresses. In his second term, President Obama had extended various protections to undocumented immigrants, and his administration prioritized deporting immigrants with a criminal felony record. Consequently, the impact of pessimism, fear, and anger on an immigrant's general faith in national policymaking institutions may have been more modest in the final months of the Obama administration, especially in comparison to the summer of 2017, when the government in Washington was much more closely identified with an anti-immigrant nativist agenda. At that point, the civic stresses gauged in the LINES surveys could be more readily traced to threats and postures from the White House. In this context, there would have been a straighter line between an immigrant's negative emotional feelings and increased wariness of federal authorities.

A second qualification has to do with a well-recognized tendency among immigrants to be perhaps inordinately upbeat about American political institutions. Although it may strike readers as counterintuitive, given the social, economic, and political marginalization that many immigrants face, that the foreign-born tend to trust government more than the native-born, surveys generally find this to be the case. Melissa Michelson reports, for example, that one-quarter of the Mexican immigrants who participated in the 1989–1990 Latino National Political Survey thought that U.S. policymakers "just about always" did what was right, and over three-quarters believed that the government was run "for the benefit of all the people," as opposed to benefiting "only a few." Among native-born Mexican Americans, these percentages were quite a bit lower: only 7 percent trusted policymakers just about always, and fewer than half (48 percent) stated that government serves all of the people.[11] Comparative research on trust and confidence in government across other Western democracies shows that this is not a distinctive American phenomenon. Overall, immigrants who settle in an industrialized democracy tend to hold that country's political institutions in higher regard than do individuals who were born there.[12]

What accounts for such a positive glow? Immigrants who settle in the United States or another democracy may arrive with relatively low expectations for government performance, given their experiences prior to migration. In many of the major migrant-sending nations in the developing world—Mexico, El Salvador, Guatemala, Honduras, the Dominican Republic, China, India, and Pakistan, among others—corruption in politics is an all-too-common feature of civic life, as is administrative mismanagement and outright repression. Anyone who grew up in such a system might look fondly at political institutions in the United States, Canada, and Western Europe regardless of the actual performance of incumbent officeholders.

Furthermore, classic "cognitive dissonance" theory could also explain why migrants tend to express great faith in the political institutions of their adoptive country.[13] The act of migration is extraordinarily costly and disruptive in both material and psychological terms. Holding the government of the receiving country in high esteem even in troubled times would be one way to justify to oneself and others the decision to emigrate. As a consequence, the "rose-colored glasses" that might be worn by default when evaluating the trustworthiness and integrity of government officials may never come off. If so, anxieties, pessimism, and anger about political figures and policies would not lead to a rise in the kind of healthy skepticism about government that a well-functioning "Madisonian" system of representation rests upon.

To expand this hypothesis, it may instead be the case that the connection between civic stress and increasing wariness of federal authorities depends on an immigrant's level of exposure to American politics. As the years since settlement pass, political practices in the country of origin may become less and less relevant for benchmarking expectations for the U.S. government, and any cognitive dissonance that an immigrant feels when questioning the trustworthiness of lawmakers could lessen. The tint of the rose-colored glasses may fade over time.

Immigrants who have gone through the process of naturalization to become American citizens could similarly feel freer to question their faith in governing institutions during politically stressful times. Being a citizen means having the wherewithal to express dissent—this is one of the core themes covered in the naturalization test, and it is a principle that would be familiar to any U.S.-born grammar school student. Given their lack of formal standing as members of the "voting public," immigrants without citizenship rights may well hold back from questioning the integrity of officials and political institutions even when emotionally burdened by government's policies and postures. That is, concerns about the well-being of friends and family members, about the direction of the country, and about the president himself could have an outsized impact among citizens who have an acknowledged right—and perhaps a subjectively felt sense of civic duty—to judge the trustworthiness and performance of government officials.

In a related way, foreign-born Latinos living in states that have passed more "pro-immigrant" statutes (such as issuing driver's licenses to undocumented immigrants) than "anti-immigrant" statutes (for example, mandatory immigration checks when individuals are detained by authorities) would have greater standing and respect within their immediate community relative to immigrants living in less-welcoming states. This recognition is of course not tantamount to the rights bestowed by citizenship. But it could translate into a heightened assertiveness in questioning the legitimacy of government officials and institutions when feeling dissatisfied or at risk.

Next we explore the dynamics of political legitimacy and the impact of civic stresses within the Latino immigrant population.

Survey Findings

The degree of faith that immigrants place in American government is captured through versions of the three questions that led off this chapter:

1. *How much of the time do you think you can trust the government in Washington to do what is right—just about always, most of the time, or only some of the time?* (When respondents volunteered "never" without prompting, this was recorded as well.)
2. *Would you say the government in Washington is pretty much run by a few big interests looking out for themselves or that it is run for the benefit of all people?*
3. *How many people running the government in Washington are corrupt— all, most, about half, a few, or none?*

Faith in government is analyzed here through three survey items, since such faith is an inherently diffuse phenomenon that could be difficult to capture in a single question. The first question taps into the presence or absence of trust, which is a sensible place to start. If immigrants are reluctant to place much trust in government, however, this could suggest either active distrust of political authorities or general uncertainty about the intentions of officials.[14] The second question, on "big interests," more directly gauges perceptions of these intentions, while the question about corruption captures suspicions of moral failings and lawbreaking.[15] Taken together, we would expect these three complementary questions to move more or less in sync over time as immigrants react to changing political climates.

The findings reported in figures 3.1, 3.2, and 3.3 offer a first cut at these dynamics. Figure 3.1 shows the aggregate distribution of trust in government among foreign-born Latinos in four very different moments—during the fall campaign of 2012, and the three waves of the 2016–2017 LINES panel survey.[16] In keeping with earlier studies of immigrants, we see evidence that the foreign-born tend to place the U.S. government in a more favorable light compared to the native-born. In the fall of 2012, only 6 percent of Latinos who were born in the United States believed that officials could be trusted "just about always"; an additional 30 percent indicated that government officials

Figure 3.1 *"How Often Do You Trust the U.S. Government to Do What Is Right?"*: *Responses of Native-Born and Foreign-Born Latinos, 2012, 2016, and 2017*

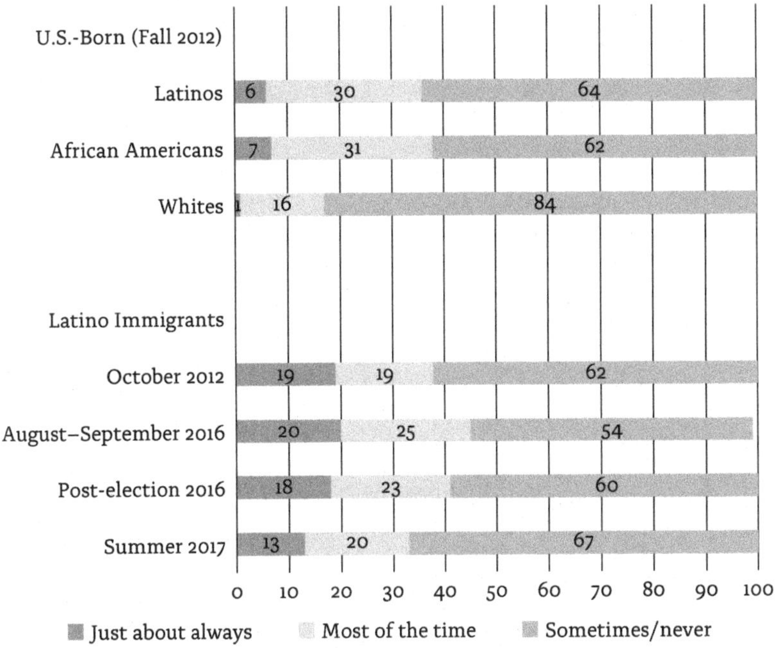

Source: 2012 American National Election Study; 2012 and 2016–2017 Latino Immigrant National Election Studies.

could be trusted "most of the time." Native-born African Americans at that time exhibited levels of trust that were similar to Latinos', while whites were appreciably more pessimistic: only 1 percent believed that government officials could be trusted all the time, and only 16 percent said they were trustworthy "most of the time." These differences across U.S.-born ethnic and racial groups are likely to stem at least in part from evaluations of incumbent officeholders at that time. Throughout the Obama years, there were persistent divides along these lines in presidential approval, with white Americans generally thinking less of the administration. By contrast, nearly one in five Latino immigrants who were interviewed in October 2012 believed that they could trust the government "just about always"—a far more robust level of faith.

Prior to the 2016 election, evaluations of governmental trustworthiness among Latino immigrants were largely unchanged from 2012.

Figure 3.2 *"Is the U.S. Government Run for Big Interests or for the Benefit of All?":*
Responses of Native-Born and Foreign-Born Latinos, 2012, 2016, and 2017

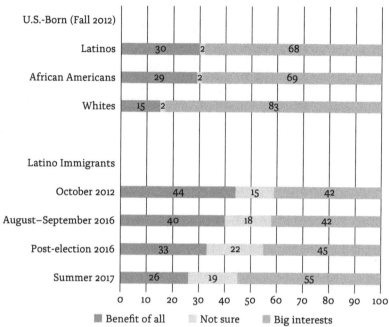

Source: 2012 American National Election Study; 2012 and 2016–2017 Latino Immigrant
National Election Studies.

The election of Donald Trump, however, ushered in a decline in faith.
By the summer of 2017, trust in the aggregate was far lower than
before the election: 67 percent of the LINES respondents indicated
then that government could be trusted only sometimes or never—
a rather pronounced margin. We must recognize, however, that at this
point in the Trump administration the signals emanating from the
White House were overwhelmingly antagonistic toward immigrants,
especially foreign-born Latinos. The fact that LINES respondents
tended to voice less trust of political authorities over time is thus
hardly surprising. But even then, the level of apprehension about
government officials did not approach that for U.S.-born whites in
the fall of 2012. One out of eight Latino immigrants in the summer
of 2017 still expressed strong trust.

Similar patterns appear in figure 3.2, which reports responses
to the "big interests" item. Three years before Donald Trump

announced his bid to seek the Republican presidential nomination, Latino immigrants were relatively sanguine about the federal government's representation of larger national interests: 44 percent of the LINES sample in October 2012 believed that government worked for the "benefit of all." Latinos who were born in the United States were decidedly less upbeat, with only 30 percent expressing this view; African American and white respondents were still more skeptical. With Trump at the top of the Republican ticket in the fall of 2016, the impression of foreign-born Latinos overall remained just as positive as in the previous election cycle. When Trump became president-elect, however, skepticism rose, and it continued to rise in the first year of his administration.

The same holds for beliefs about corruption in the federal government (figure 3.3). In the aggregate, Latino immigrants perceived more wrongdoing in high places following the 2016 election. As with the item on political trust, however, this loss of faith in governing institutions was not so profound as to match what was observed for U.S.-born Latinos, African Americans, and whites when President Obama was seeking reelection in 2012.

Taken together, these aggregate trends point to a reappraisal of the federal government that accords with our expectations. As the political winds shifted against immigrants, beliefs about the trustworthiness, fairness, and integrity of officials also shifted. The rose-colored glasses that immigrants wear when evaluating the legitimacy of American government are not so tinted as to amount to blind faith.

Moving to the individual level of analysis allows us to put a finer point on how civic stresses in the new political era contributed to declining levels of trust. When the focus turns to the continuity in responses across the three survey waves of the 2016–2017 LINES panel, we find a fair amount of attitude change, as summarized in figure 3.4. The numeric scores reported here can be thought of as continuity measures. A score of 1.0 would tell us that the distribution of attitudes in one period carried over perfectly to the next; that is, immigrants who were relatively more trusting remained so in the later survey period. On the other hand, if an immigrant's evaluation of trustworthiness and integrity in government at one point in time had no bearing whatsoever on judgments at a later period, the continuity would be recorded as zero. These continuity scores, as noted at

Figure 3.3 *"How Many of the People Running the Government in Washington Are Corrupt?": Responses of Native-Born and Foreign-Born Latinos, 2012, 2016, and 2017*

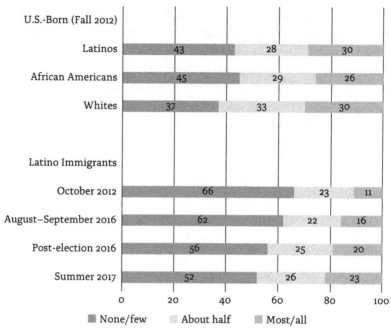

Source: 2012 American National Election Study; 2012 and 2016–2017 Latino Immigrant National Election Studies.

the bottom of figure 3.4, were calculated through regression analysis. As mentioned in the previous chapter, this is a technique for determining how well one variable predicts another.

In figure 3.4, a considerable amount of attitude change is evident. The continuity scores for each of these items are a far cry from 1.0. From the first to the second survey period, the average stability measure is under 0.30. Some of this change in attitudes no doubt stems from "top-of-the-head" considerations that were relevant before the election but did not come to mind when responding to the same items in another interview after the campaign.[17] The average stability measure linking attitudes in the second and third waves, however, is somewhat lower, at approximately 0.20. This difference in continuities across the three panel waves suggests that survey responses consist of more than simple top-of-the-head considerations. After all, if such considerations were behind fluctuations in

Figure 3.4 *Stability of Latino Immigrants' Attitudes Toward the Federal Government, 2016–2017*

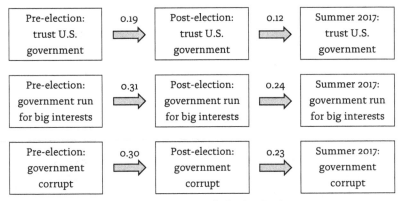

Source: 2016–2017 Latino Immigrant National Election Study.
Note: Stability coefficients were estimated via ordinary least squares regression. The standard error for each regression estimate is 0.05.

responses to the three items, we would expect to see as much change between the second and third survey periods as between the first and second. It is thus reasonable to consider the possibility that civic stress brought about a loss of faith in American government, with the most consequential effects happening between the second and third survey periods.

In figures 3.5, 3.6, and 3.7, we show the various impacts of civic stress in each time period. These effects were gauged through more extensive regression analyses. After taking into account a number of social and demographic background traits, each of the civic stress measures—pessimism about the direction that the United States was headed, a set of "dummy" variables[18] that captured negative emotional reactions to Donald Trump, worries that a close friend or family member would be deported, and anxiety about the financial well-being of the respondent's family—was added on its own to the regression model to track its effect on attitude change.[19]

Figure 3.5 presents the effect of a particular stress in civic life on perceptions of trustworthiness in government. The height of a bar reflects the average attitude change that is predicted as a given civic stress item increases from its lowest to highest value. Nearly all of these bars run in a negative direction, implying (not surprisingly) that

Figure 3.5 *Impact of Civic Stresses on Latino Immigrants' Trust in American Government, 2016–2017*

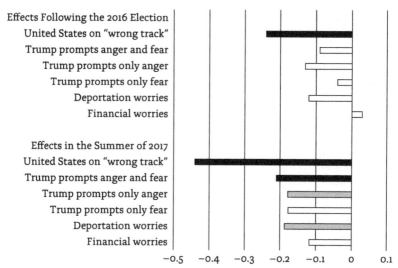

Source: 2016–2017 Latino Immigrant National Election Study.

Note: These bars show the amount of change in trust on average as a given civic stress increases from its lowest to highest value. For the dummy predictors measuring emotional reactions to Trump, the effects are benchmarked relative to not feeling angry or afraid. Light gray shading indicates statistical significance at the 0.10 level; solid black bars are significant at the 0.05 level. Civic stresses as measured in the first or second survey wave were used to predict changes in trust following the 2016 election; civic stresses gauged in the third wave were used to predict changes in trust in the summer of 2017. When calculating these impacts, an immigrant's level of trust from the preceding survey wave was taken into account, along with several personal and demographic factors (civic status, time in the United States, age, gender, education, family income, language use at home, attendance at religious services, marital status, homeownership, policy disposition toward immigrants in the state of residence, and Mexican origin, dummy-coded).

pessimism, anxieties, and anger depress faith in government. There is appreciable variation, however, in effects. To help interpret these results, we have printed statistically significant changes in solid black; an impact that approaches significance appears in gray. In the presidential transition period, pessimism about the direction that the United States was headed caused a significant decline in trust. To a much lesser (and statistically insignificant) extent, immigrants who were concerned about the possible deportation of friends or family also grew less trusting of federal authorities. Having felt afraid of Donald Trump during the campaign, anger toward him, or both anger and fear is likewise associated with declining trust, but these results are also insignificant.

Come the summer of 2017, these civic stress items became more forceful. At this juncture, the impact of pessimism concerning the direction of the United States had nearly doubled in magnitude from the transition period. Negative emotional reactions to President Trump also mattered far more. Interestingly, fear of the president did not trigger a greater loss of trust than anger. This runs contrary to some of the prior scholarly research on emotions and politics (discussed in chapter 2). The results in figure 3.5 show that immigrants' fear does indeed reduce their trust in government, though it is most potent when anger toward Trump has also been triggered. On its own, anger is also found to make immigrants less trusting. Immigrants in the summer of 2017 who worried that a friend or family member would be deported became similarly less trusting than they had been during the presidential transition period.

Turning to the item on whether the federal government is run for the benefit of all or only for the "big interests," a comparable pattern emerges (figure 3.6). In the model of attitude change between the pre-election and transitional periods, the items on civic stress matter relatively little. Only concerns that the United States is on the "wrong track" had a statistically significant impact on judgments. The civic stress items carried far more weight in the later time period: all save the question about financial worries raised suspicions about the government. The impact of pessimism about the direction of the country was particularly strong. All things equal, the analysis here suggests that the probability of believing that "big interests" controlled the government would be 0.24 higher for an immigrant who thought that the country was moving in the wrong direction relative to those who were satisfied with where the country was headed—a very large effect indeed.

For the item on corruption (figure 3.7), the strongest and most significant effect again surfaces in the summer of 2017. At this time, immigrants who were disappointed in the direction that the country had taken became more suspicious of wrongdoing in high places. While this effect overshadows that of the other items on anxiety

Figure 3.6 *Impact of Civic Stresses on Latino Immigrants' Belief That Government Is Run for "Big Interests," 2016–2017*

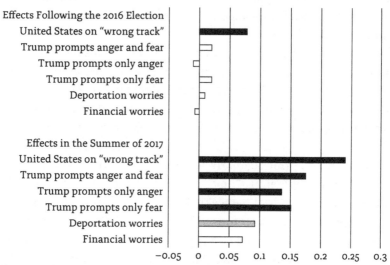

Source: 2016–2017 Latino Immigrant National Election Study.

Note: These bars show the change in probability of believing that "big interests" run the government as a given civic stress item increases from its lowest to highest value. Light gray shading indicates statistical significance at the 0.10 level; solid black bars are significant at the 0.05 level. Civic stresses as measured in the first or second survey wave were used to predict attitude changes following the 2016 election; civic stressors gauged in the third wave were used to predict attitude changes in the summer of 2017. When calculating these impacts, an immigrant's belief about "big interests" from the preceding survey wave was taken into account, along with several personal and demographic factors (civic status, time in the United States, age, gender, education, family income, language use at home, attendance at religious services, marital status, homeownership, policy disposition toward immigrants in the state of residence, and Mexican origin, dummy-coded).

and anger, the results in this figure complement those for general trust in government and beliefs about whether officials truly work for the benefit of everyone in the country. Taken together, the charts in figures 3.4 through 3.7 demonstrate, first, that faith in American representative institutions is highly dynamic; and second, that the stresses of civic life—both concerns about the country and its principal leader and concerns about the well-being of those within respondents' immediate social networks—cause immigrants to question the legitimacy of governing authorities.

Figure 3.7 *Impact of Civic Stresses on Latino Immigrants' Impressions of Corruption in the Federal Government, 2016–2017*

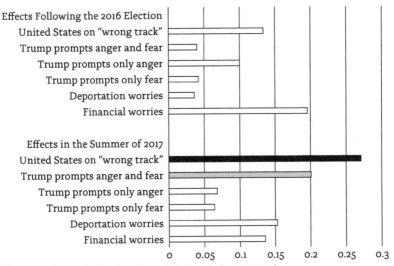

Source: 2016–2017 Latino Immigrant National Election Study.

Note: These bars show the average amount of attitude change as a given civic stress item increases from its lowest to highest value. Light gray shading indicates statistical significance at the 0.10 level; the solid black bar is significant at the 0.05 level. Civic stresses as measured in the first or second survey wave were used to predict attitude changes following the 2016 election; civic stresses gauged in the third wave were used to predict attitude changes in the summer of 2017. When calculating these impacts, an immigrant's belief about corruption in government from the preceding survey wave was taken into account, along with several personal and demographic factors (civic status, time in the United States, age, gender, education, family income, language use at home, attendance at religious services, marital status, homeownership, policy disposition toward immigrants in the state of residence, and Mexican origin, dummy-coded).

How do these patterns vary depending on how much exposure immigrants have had to American politics, whether or not they have been formally integrated into the electorate through naturalization, whether or not they live in a more welcoming state, and whether or not they are Mexican-born? As noted earlier, previous research has found that the longer an immigrant has lived in the United States, the lighter the tint in the rose-colored glasses when evaluating governing institutions. Naturalization is also, perhaps paradoxically, linked to diminished faith in American government. To extend this line of reasoning, we raised the possibility earlier that the impact of political pessimism, anxiety, and anger could be greater on immigrants who have deeper experience in the United States or a more formal standing from which to register claims against the government.

We can assess such variations through statistical interactions. For all of the regression models from which the results presented in figures 3.5 to 3.7 were derived, each civic stress item was allowed to interact with the number of years the respondent had lived in the United States. Then in a second set of models, interaction terms based on naturalization status were evaluated. We next explored interactions between each civic stress item and the policy climate toward immigrants within the respondent's state of residence. Finally, we examined whether the effects of any of the civic stress items varied based on national origin (Mexicans versus non-Mexicans).[20] The results from these analyses show that such interactions were few and far between.

In fact, only one statistically significant interaction surfaced, which is displayed in figure 3.8. In the summer of 2017, pessimism concerning the direction that the United States had taken influenced the perceived trustworthiness of the federal government to a somewhat larger degree for immigrants who had resided in the country for a longer period of time. This figure illustrates this distinction. For immigrants who had lived in the United States for thirty-five years, the average impact was a drop in governmental trust by more than half a point. For relative newcomers—portrayed in figure 3.8 as immigrants with only fifteen years of residence in the country—the effect of evaluations of where the country was heading was just over half as large. This significant interaction result was not replicated in models of whether the government serves "big interests" and whether corruption is widespread. Nor did any significant interactions appear when the effects of the different civic stress items were allowed to vary by naturalization status or policy disposition toward immigrants in the state of residence.

There is thus quite limited support for the notion that rose-colored glasses more readily come off when naturalized citizens, longer-term residents, and immigrants living in more welcoming states who are burdened by civic stresses like those surrounding the 2016 elections

Figure 3.8 *Effect of Pessimism About the Direction Being Taken by the United States on Latino Immigrants' Trust in American Government, by Length of Residence in the Country, Summer 2017*

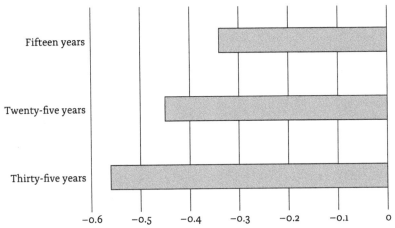

Source: 2016–2017 Latino Immigrant National Election Study.

Note: Bars represent the average amount of change in trust levels from the second to third panel wave, as predicted through a multivariate regression, with the personal and demographic factors used in earlier models taken into account. The interaction between evaluations of the direction of the country and time spent in the United States is statistically significant.

evaluate the trustworthiness, fairness, and integrity of the U.S. government. Foreign-born Latinos in general question their faith in federal authorities when they feel politically pessimistic, anxious, or angry, and skepticism became particularly pronounced with Donald Trump in the White House. The larger implications of these patterns for the incorporation of immigrants into American democracy can be explored by examining just how far this loss of faith spreads. We turn to this analysis in the next chapter.

IMMIGRANT ATTACHMENTS TO AMERICAN SOCIETY   4

HOLDING FAST?

On October 20, 1961, the *Federal Register* published a fresh administrative protocol concerning the removal of immigrants who had been ordered by a court to leave the United States. Any such immigrant could, with the approval of authorities, "deport himself at his own expense and to a destination of his own choice." Should this occur, the immigrant "shall be considered to have been deported in pursuance of law."[1] This provision of federal immigration law has been revised various times and remains on the books, with cases of repatriation in this way commonly grouped under the heading of "voluntary departure" (as opposed to "involuntary separation"). When the protocol was first announced, however, it was characterized as "self-deportation."

We suspect that many Americans are familiar with the phrase "self-deportation." But we also suspect that this phrase is not usually understood in narrow administrative terms, per the *Federal Register*. Rather, over the years, as lawmakers have wrestled with immigration policy reforms, the notion of self-deportation has come to refer to a decision immigrants might make when it becomes increasingly difficult to find employment and housing, obtain medical care, and generally look out for themselves and their families. As the stresses and strains of everyday life build up, these immigrants may opt simply to exit the country—to "deport" themselves, in a manner of speaking—regardless of any contacts with judicial officials or administrative orders.

In his reelection campaign of 1994, Governor Pete Wilson of California became most closely identified with this broader, non-judicial understanding of self-deportation, making it a key element in his policy agenda. During a CNN interview, the Republican governor called for denying health care and educational services to undocumented immigrants, so as to reduce their number in the state. "I think you'd see self-deportation," Wilson argued, "because life here would not be very attractive."[2] At that time, the governor's proposal was exceedingly controversial, both within his own political party and with the public on the whole. The columnist William Safire, a former speechwriter in the Nixon White House who remained influential in Republican circles, spoke for many when he questioned the morality, achievability, and wisdom of a policy of self-deportation. As Safire put it in an op-ed:

> What's Wilson's purpose in all this? . . . Make 'em so miserable that they leave the country. . . . Would we rather have 300,000 children on the streets, learning costly delinquency—or safely in school, becoming potential citizens and taxpayers? . . . [A] government policy of making any child's life miserable is . . . an abomination.[3]

Governor Wilson was successful in his reelection bid, but his plan to deny state services to immigrants largely failed owing to challenges in court. In late 1994, a federal district judge ruled that it would be unconstitutional for firefighters, police officers, medical professionals, and teachers to inquire about immigration status before providing services to a resident, a decision that struck at the heart of the "self-deportation" strategy. This ruling was upheld in later judicial opinions, and in the years since the Wilson administration California has moved in the opposite direction on immigrant rights, enacting a set of more welcoming policies on access to education, health care, and other public services. The Democratic Party is now the dominant force in statewide elections, and as seen in figure 2.5, California today is among the most immigrant-friendly states in the country.

This legacy of the Wilson years notwithstanding, proposals to address the challenges of migration through policies to encourage self-deportation have continued to come up in more recent political campaigns. Most notably, in a Republican presidential primary debate in January 2012, Mitt Romney embraced the concept. In response to a question on immigration, the eventual nominee referred to steps he would take as president to verify the legal eligibility of workers in the United States and then remarked: "If people don't get work here, they're going to self-deport to a place they can get work."[4] Four years later, in a similar Republican presidential primary debate, then-candidate Donald Trump predicted that such self-deporting would be a natural consequence of the tougher enforcement policies he advocated. "'Self-deportation' is people are going to leave as soon as they see others going out."[5]

In this chapter, we take a close look at self-deportation from the perspective of immigrants themselves. Do the civic stresses related to deportation, financial woes, misgivings about the direction of the country, and the actions of Donald Trump cause immigrants to doubt whether they should remain in the United States over the long run? The tumultuous and polarizing political environment following the 2016 elections allows us to probe what might be labeled the "self-deportation" hypothesis in ways that have not been previously examined. When exploring the effects of political pessimism, worries, and anger, we assess both a potential "hard" exit from the United States, in the form of making plans to return to one's country of origin, and the "softer" kind of exit indicated by psychological estrangement from American society—trusting Americans less, or feeling less of an emotional attachment to the country.

Findings from the LINES survey speak to the title of this book: Latino immigrants are "holding fast." The evidence tells us that foreign-born Latinos who are burdened by various civic stresses are not pulling back from U.S. society: most are neither contemplating a "hard" exit nor becoming disenchanted with Americans and America. Before moving to these results, we provide a fuller theoretical backdrop for this analysis.

Theoretical Backdrop

A core premise of much of the research on the forces that prompt international migration is that the decision to emigrate from one's country of birth is rooted in prospective hunches about expected gains or losses. People considering whether or not to leave their country in search of better opportunities abroad calculate as well as possible their likely gains after settlement and compare this potential outcome to their anticipated quality of life should they stay in place. Microeconomists label this an "expected utility" model of decision-making: choice options are evaluated based on potential benefits and costs, and then the course of action that elicits the greatest payoff in the foreseeable future is chosen.[6] Of course, there are many factors that influence the movement of migrants from one country to another, some of which may not be related to any reckoning of future payoffs. But the premise that cost-benefit calculations are behind decisions about where to live, what kinds of employment to pursue, and what kinds of risks are worth taking is a useful starting point for studying what drives the choice to migrate.

All things equal, we would anticipate that any factors that diminish the expected benefits from settling in the United States—say, difficulties in finding work, or concerns about the well-being of friends and family—could dampen enthusiasm for staying in the country. There is a certain plausible logic behind the anti-immigrant self-deportation arguments that Pete Wilson, Mitt Romney, and Donald Trump put forth. Anecdotally, service professionals and advocates who work in immigrant communities have wondered whether rising tensions after the 2016 elections have sparked a wave of return migration. For instance, Muzaffer Chishti, the director of the Migration Policy Institute at the New York University School of Law, remarked in April 2018, with respect to undocumented immigrants in particular, that "people are making plans to leave, people are making plans to sell their house, people are making plans—if eventually [they] leave [their] children behind, who should get their guardianship, what should happen to their school, to their bank accounts?" At the same time, this commentator noted that "tracking the number of people who leave on their own . . . is nearly impossible."[7]

Chishti's comments speak to the costliness of uprooting oneself after becoming established in a new community. It would be difficult to specify in the abstract how much harder life must become for an immigrant to justify making concrete plans to exit. It seems reasonable to suppose, however, that it would take a considerable amount of hardship and apprehensiveness to prompt such planning, along with a good deal of confidence that life in one's native country would be appreciably better upon return. The stresses of the current political climate may consequently have only modest effects in the aggregate. A few years before the incoming Trump administration, Senator Marco Rubio of Florida, speaking on the floor of the U.S. Senate on

June 11, 2013, anticipated as much. "[We can try to] make life so tough on people that they'll just leave on their own. I don't think that's a practical approach. I don't think it works. . . . They'll figure out a way to survive and endure."[8]

In-depth focus-group discussions with Mexican immigrants conducted by Carmen Valez and her colleagues in Arizona just after the state passed landmark anti-immigrant legislation in 2010 bolster the claim of Senator Rubio.[9] Arizona Senate Bill 1070 required police officers to determine the immigration status of anyone who was stopped if they suspected that the detainee was undocumented. The law also imposed penalties on individuals who were housing, hiring, or transporting undocumented immigrants. Critics charged that such measures invited racial profiling and arbitrary arrests. Many of the Mexicans in the focus groups were mindful of the increasing hostility toward immigrants across the state at that moment and were not blind to the risks they faced when going about their day-to-day activities. At the same time, repatriation was not a desirable option because returning to Mexico would also be fraught with risks and uncertainties. Many also cited family and community connections that were sources of support and comfort in hard times. One focus-group participant explained, "I know a lot of people here. If I can't find a job through one friend, I'd call another and so on." Another participant shared that "I have all my grandchildren and others here. I could never return." These kinds of connections take time to develop, of course, but as Marco Rubio surmised, even in a hostile climate, these immigrants were finding ways to survive and endure.[10]

For our part, we were able to track the dynamics of repatriation planning within a large cohort of Latin America–born immigrants across the politically turbulent period around the 2016 elections. When analyzing the effects of civic stresses on plans to repatriate, we probe variations based on how long an immigrant has lived in the United States. We also assess whether immigrants who were not naturalized citizens or green-card-holders, immigrants who lived in less welcoming states, or Mexicans in particular were especially inclined to consider returning to their country of origin when feeling pessimistic, anxious, or angry.

Doubting whether one truly belongs in the United States over the long run could undermine trajectories of incorporation into

American democracy. Immigrants who are considering repatriating may see little reason to learn about politics in the United States and take part. Along similar lines, the "softer" forms of withdrawal—placing less trust in Americans or holding the United States on the whole in lower esteem—could be corrosive as well for democratic incorporation. Within the wider electorate, interpersonal trust and an abiding sense of patriotism have long been linked to political engagement.[11] We saw in the preceding chapter that civic stresses exerted powerful effects on judgments about the trustworthiness and integrity of U.S. government officials and institutions. Do these effects extend broadly to implicate Americans across the board and the country itself?

If so, this would be a troubling finding that points toward deeper-seated political alienation. Recall, however, from the analysis of immigrants' changing faith in government that the impact of civic stress was largely confined to the post-transition period. Once Donald Trump became president, there would have been a clear connection between the political postures of the federal government and the kinds of civic stresses that many immigrants were experiencing—the connection would at least have been clearer than under the Obama administration. This distinction from the previous chapter suggests that the effects of political pessimism, anxiety, and anger would not be so diffuse as to turn immigrants away from American society at large, even if they grew suspicious of governing institutions under Trump.

Findings from the U.S. Census and LINES Surveys

Upon taking office, Donald Trump sought to implement the anti-immigrant policies on which he campaigned. His administration was stymied in many of these initiatives, but Trump's goal as president was clear: to reorient federal immigration policy. Using whatever levers were available, he aimed to put up administrative roadblocks to migrant and refugee settlement while encouraging greater repatriation among those who were already in the country. With respect to this latter objective, is there evidence to suggest that immigrants became more open to self-deportation following the 2016 election?

In the aggregate, the outcome of this election does not seem to have prompted hasty widespread departures. According to census data

Figure 4.1 *Number of Immigrants (in Millions) in the United States, 2005–2018*

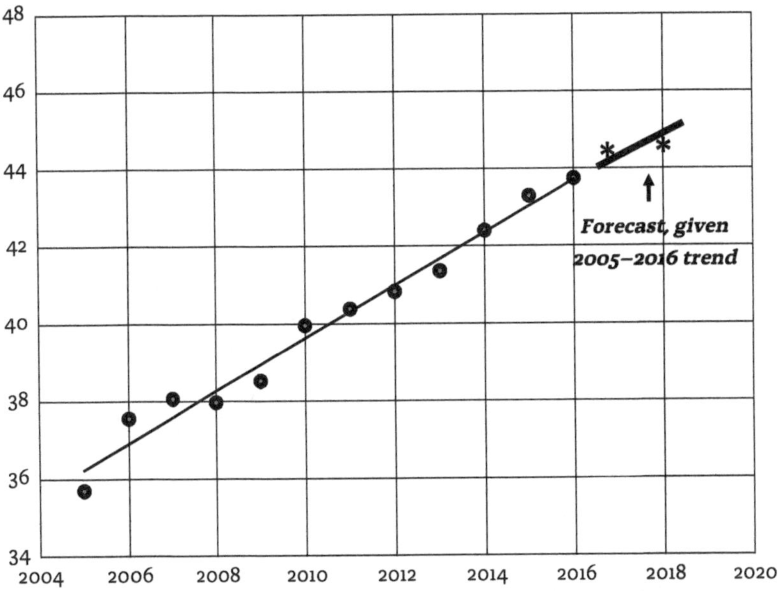

Source: U.S. Census Bureau American Community Surveys (which began in 2005). *Note:* The trend line was calculated via ordinary least squares regression (b = .68, R^2 = 0.98, N = 12 years). Asterisks indicate the size of the foreign-born population as reported in the ACS: 44.53 million in 2017 and 44.73 million in 2018. The linear trend from 2005 to 2016 predicts 44.41 million immigrants in 2017 (with a 95 percent confidence interval range from 43.90 to 44.88) and 45.09 million in 2018 (95 percent confidence interval range from 44.52 to 45.62).

published in the American Community Survey (ACS), an estimated 44.73 million immigrants lived in the United States in 2018, the most recent year in which records are available. This figure represents an increase of approximately one million since 2016. An expansion such as this fits with historic trends in the foreign-born population count, as shown in figure 4.1. Between 2005 and 2016, the size of the immigrant population grew by approximately eight million. This growth was fairly steady year by year; a linear trend calculated through ordinary least squares regression captures this increase well.[12] With each passing year, approximately 700,000 more immigrants on average were added annually to the overall foreign-born population. Based on this trend line, we would have expected 44.41 million immigrants to be living in the country in 2017 (with a 95 percent confidence

Figure 4.2 *Long-Term Residential Plans of Latino Immigrants, 2005–2017*

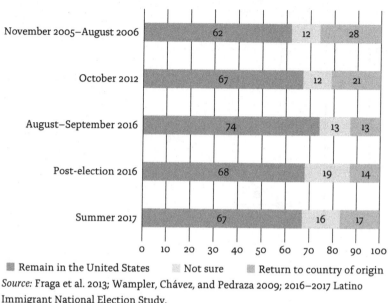

Remain in the United States ▪ Not sure ▪ Return to country of origin

Source: Fraga et al. 2013; Wampler, Chávez, and Pedraza 2009; 2016–2017 Latino Immigrant National Election Study.

interval of 43.90 to 44.88) and 45.09 million in 2018 (with a 95 percent confidence interval of 44.52 to 45.62). In fact, the ACS puts these figures at 44.53 and 44.73 million, respectively. What this indicates is that evidently there was no immediate and significant contraction of the immigrant population in the wake of the 2016 election.[13] This does not necessarily contradict the self-deportation hypothesis, but such population increases would certainly have been less likely if large numbers of previously settled immigrants began heading for the doors in 2017.

Surveys of immigrants conducted at different points in time provide greater leverage to assess how decisions to remain in the United States or repatriate varied as political climates changed. Figure 4.2 presents comparative evidence along these lines. From late 2005 through mid-2006, 5,563 Latin America–born immigrants were interviewed as part of the Latino National Survey.[14] These respondents were asked whether or not they had plans to go back to their country of origin. Nearly two out of three (62 percent) indicated that they had no such plans, a percentage that matches that found in a 2003 survey of seasonal Mexican-born farmworkers in the American

West.[15] The implication is that the two-out-of-three margin for wishing to remain permanently in the United States could be widely generalized across the Latino immigrant population, at least for that particular time period in the early to mid-2000s.

Several years later, two-thirds of the respondents in the 2012 Latino Immigrant National Election Study reported an intention to stay in the United States. Only one out of five expressed an intention to return to their country of origin. Come the summer of 2016, there was an even greater commitment among immigrants to remain. At this juncture, 74 percent stated that they had no plans to leave. Following the election of Donald Trump, however, this percentage dropped back down to its pre-2016 level—a noteworthy if not substantial decline that we investigate later in this chapter.[16] At the conclusion of the 2016–2017 LINES panel, the overall distribution of those intending to remain versus those intending to return was essentially the same as during the presidential transition period.

In general, immigrants who were not naturalized citizens or legal permanent residents (green-card-holders) were less apt to say that they wanted to remain in the United States permanently. The same was true for those who had spent relatively less time in United States. Quite understandably, the longer an immigrant has lived in the country, the more deeply rooted he or she is likely to be. As the political climate became less welcoming for foreign-born Latinos, one might expect that LINES respondents who were not citizens or green-card-holders would become especially open to considering self-deportation, as would those with less experience in the country. When Governor Wilson, Governor (now Senator) Romney, President Trump, and other proponents of self-deportation policies have spoken of this strategy, they typically single out these groups as their principal targets.

As noted in the second chapter, within the 2016–2017 LINES sample, the average length of time residing in the United States was approximately twenty-three years. In a follow-up to figure 4.2, figure 4.3 shows the long-term residential plans in 2016 and 2017 of Latino immigrants who were noncitizens without green cards, those who had lived in the United States for only fifteen years, those who had lived in a state where strongly restrictive statutes against immigrants were on the books, and those who had emigrated from

Figure 4.3 *Long-Term Residential Plans of Latino Immigrants, 2016–2017*

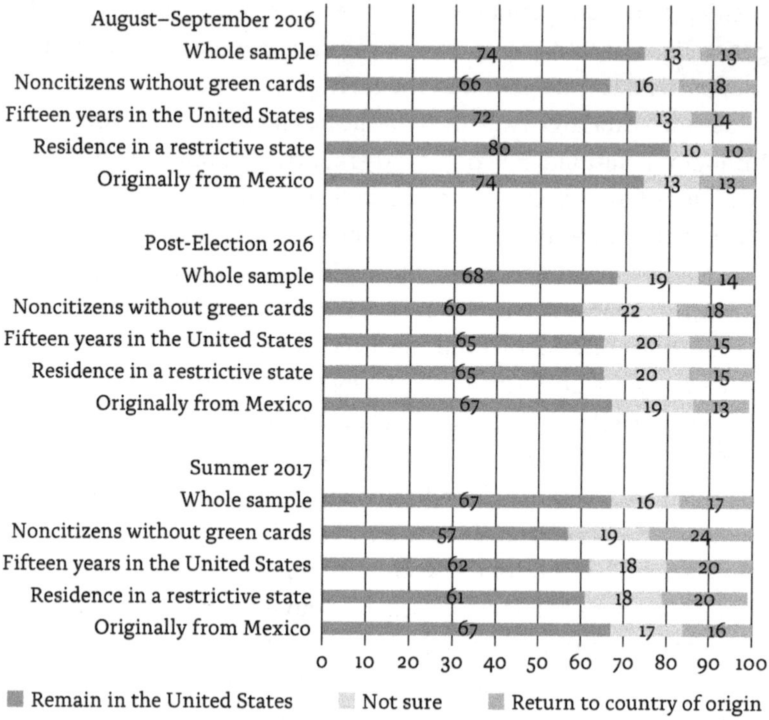

August–September 2016		
Whole sample	74 / 13 / 13
Noncitizens without green cards	66 / 16 / 18
Fifteen years in the United States	72 / 13 / 14
Residence in a restrictive state	80 / 10 / 10
Originally from Mexico	74 / 13 / 13
Post-Election 2016		
Whole sample	68 / 19 / 14
Noncitizens without green cards	60 / 22 / 18
Fifteen years in the United States	65 / 20 / 15
Residence in a restrictive state	65 / 20 / 15
Originally from Mexico	67 / 19 / 13
Summer 2017		
Whole sample	67 / 16 / 17
Noncitizens without green cards	57 / 19 / 24
Fifteen years in the United States	62 / 18 / 20
Residence in a restrictive state	61 / 18 / 20
Originally from Mexico	67 / 17 / 16

■ Remain in the United States ▨ Not sure ▨ Return to country of origin

Source: 2016–2017 Latino Immigrant National Election Study.

Note: The percentages for fifteen years of residence in the United States and residence in a restrictive state are estimates based on ordinal logistic regression analyses. In one model, long-term residential plans were regressed on time spent in the country; in another model, long-term residential plans were regressed on the state-level immigration policy disposition scale in figure 2.5. For illustrative purposes, a "restrictive" state is one that scored –5 on this scale, the lowest possible value.

Mexico. Immediately after the 2016 election, the number of immigrants in each subgroup who intended to remain indefinitely in the country dropped, as it did for the sample on the whole. Attitude shifts for the four subgroups were larger relative to the entire sample, but only slightly larger. Before the election, 66 percent of immigrants without citizenship or a green card anticipated remaining in the country permanently. In the presidential transition period, this dropped to 60 percent. For respondents who had lived in the United States for fifteen years, this figure decreased from 72 to 65 percent.

A somewhat larger drop was found for immigrants who lived in unwelcoming states. Before the election, an estimated 80 percent of this group wished to remain indefinitely in the United States; this percentage decreased to 65 percent during the post-election transition period. Such attitude changes merit further scrutiny. As for the whole sample, the breakdown of residential plans for these subgroups of respondents changed little between the presidential transition wave and the summer of 2017. The minor uptick in the aggregate in inclinations to "self-deport" occurred right after the election of Donald Trump but was short-lived.

If we probe more deeply to examine how many LINES respondents changed their plans over the course of the panel survey, we find a fair amount of stability in preferences. Among the immigrants in the pre-election period who stated that they intended to remain in the United States—74 percent of the entire sample—only 8 percent indicated that they had plans to leave when interviewed again during the presidential transition period. Another 16 percent of these immigrants moved to the "not sure" column. We thus observe some limited disenchantment with life in the United States right after the election, not a major rush to the doors. Between the second and third survey waves, there was a similar degree of continuity in long-term plans. In the second wave, 68 percent of respondents reported having no plans to exit the country. Come the summer of 2017, only 10 percent of these immigrants mentioned having new plans to leave, and 14 percent changed their response to "not sure." Again, not a major rush to the doors. These changes were offset to an extent by immigrants who stated in one period that they were planning to exit but then in a subsequent survey wave indicated that they were not sure about departing or no longer had such plans.[17] Although there was significant continuity over time in long-term residential preferences, these changes in responses are nevertheless worth a close look. Did pessimism about the direction that the country was going at a particular juncture, anxiety or anger about Donald Trump, concerns that a family member or friend would be deported, or worries about family finances trigger such updating?

As before, we probe this question through regression analysis, where a particular civic stress item predicts long-term residential plans after taking into account the plan that the respondent expressed in the previous survey wave.[18] The results from these analyses are decidedly underwhelming. In the presidential transition period, none of the civic stress items had a statistically significant impact on long-term plans to remain in the United States or leave, though fears about the deportation of friends or family members came close to being significant ($p = .11$). Such concerns led to an increase of four percentage points in the number of immigrants mentioning a plan to leave when interviewed right after the election. When surveyed again in the summer of 2017, respondents provided even less evidence that the four civic stress items were linked to their long-term residential planning. The effects of pessimism, negative emotional reactions to President Trump, and worries about deportations or family finances were all quite insignificant.

These findings stand in great contrast to those uncovered in the previous chapter, where all of the civic stress items were found to have triggered a loss of faith in American government. By the summer of 2017, the burdens and misgivings felt by Latino immigrants six months into the Trump era did not prompt thoughts of self-deportation. As Marco Rubio posited in 2013, even when life became tougher, immigrants on the whole did not grow more prone to "just leave on their own." This held as well for immigrants who were not naturalized citizens or legal permanent residents, for immigrants who were relative newcomers to the country, for immigrants who lived in a state where many restrictive anti-immigrant measures had been enacted, and for Mexicans and non-Mexicans alike. When each of the civic stress measures is allowed to interact with civic status, the number of years spent in the United States, state policy disposition toward immigrants, or national origin (Mexico versus another country), no noteworthy and significant variations in effects come up. Immigrants who were less well established in the country were no more likely than others to contemplate repatriating in response to civic stresses during either the presidential transition period or the following summer.

The fact that these civic stress items have influenced thoughts about repatriation so little is strong evidence against the self-deportation hypothesis. To explore this hypothesis further, we turn to the Pew Research Center's National Survey of Latinos fielded in the summer of 2018.[19] In this study, 720 foreign-born Latinos were queried about whether, if they could do it again, they would opt to stay in their country of birth, emigrate to the United States, or go to a different country. This item is not the same as the LINES question about prospective planning, but it taps into the same mindset. And the proportion of immigrants indicating that they would settle in the United States all over again, 73 percent, is roughly comparable to the margin of LINES respondents who reported having no plans to leave the United States.

The Pew survey also asked about respondents' level of anxiety about deportation—a question comparable to similar questions in the LINES study. When asked in 2018 how worried they were that they, a family member, or a close friend would be deported, only 21 percent said that they were not at all worried. At the other end of this scale, 35 percent expressed a lot of worry. Given the political climate when this poll was taken, these concerns are understandable. However, as seen in figure 4.4, such worries did not correlate with second-guessing their decision to come to the United States in the first place. Immigrants who voiced a great deal of anxiety about deportations were on the whole as satisfied with their decision to emigrate as those who were not worried. The takeaway here is that within the Latino immigrant community, even among those in the United States without papers, attachments to the United States run deep.

What about a "softer" decoupling from the country amid the civic stresses of the post-election environment? Although there is little evidence that Latin America–born immigrants planned to leave the country in greater numbers, and the foreign-born population on the whole was keeping pace with its historic trajectory, Latino immigrants may have become more guarded about Americans and less emotionally attached to the country overall. In the 2012 American National Election Study and the LINES surveys from 2012 and 2016–2017, respondents were asked to judge the trustworthiness of other people in the United States—whether Americans could always be trusted, trusted most of the time, trusted only half of the time, only sometimes trusted, or never trusted. Comparisons of responses to this item are given in figure 4.5.

Among the U.S.-born in 2012, we observe an appreciable amount of variation in interpersonal trust. Ethnic minorities (Latinos and African Americans) were somewhat less confident in others compared

Figure 4.4 *"If You Could Do It Again, Would You Come to the United States, Stay in the Country Where You Were Born, or Go to a Different Country?": Latino Immigrants' Attitudes About Emigration by Worries About Deportations, Summer 2018*

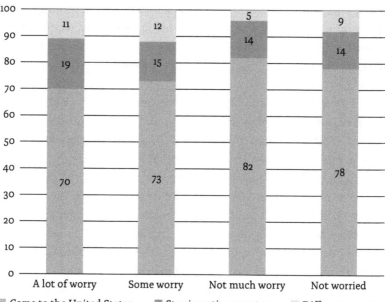

Come to the United States   Stay in native country   Different country

Source: 2018 Pew Hispanic Center National Survey of Latinos.
Note: Weighted N = 720 foreign-born Latinos over age eighteen. Surveys were conducted between July 26 and September 9, 2018. Thirty-five percent expressed "a lot of worry" that they, a family member, or a close friend would be deported; 32 percent had "some worry"; 12 percent were "not much worried"; and 21 percent were "not at all worried." $\chi^2_6 = 6.05$, $p = .42$.

to U.S.-born whites. This difference across ethnic groups has been much discussed in earlier research.[20] As members of groups that are more socially and economically marginalized, U.S.-born Latinos and African Americans generally experience more discrimination and political exclusion throughout their lives than whites, and that can lead to a certain cautiousness when interacting with others. For their part, Latino immigrants in 2012 voiced opinions that were less trusting compared to U.S.-born Latinos, but they were also less distrusting. Latino immigrants tended to fall along the midpoint of this scale: 44 percent stated that Americans could be trusted about half of the time.

Among these immigrants, a pattern emerges from 2012 to 2017 that is similar to that found for repatriation planning. LINES respondents

Figure 4.5 *"How Often Can You Trust Other People in the United States?": Levels of Interpersonal Trust Among U.S.-Born Latinos, African Americans, and Whites in the Fall of 2012 and Latino Immigrants, 2012 and 2016–2017*

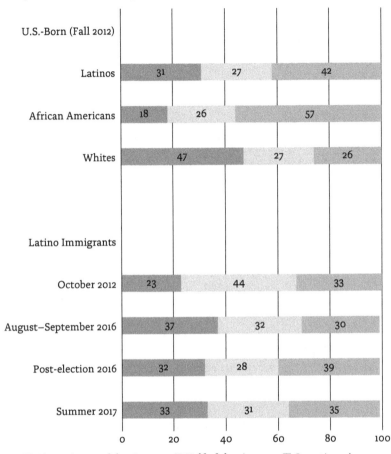

Source: 2012 American National Election Study; 2012 and 2016–2017 Latino Immigrant National Election Studies.

before the 2016 election were more inclined than in 2012 to trust Americans. Approximately one-third (37 percent) stated that they trusted other people all or most of the time, which was fifteen points higher than the margin in October 2012. There was a slight decrease in trust following the election of Donald Trump, and this dip carried over to the summer of 2017. At that point, 33 percent were highly trusting, while 35 percent expressed little or no trust. As with preferences for

Figure 4.6 *"When You See the American Flag Flying, How Do You Feel?":*
U.S.-Centric Patriotism Among Latino Immigrants, 2012 and 2016–2017

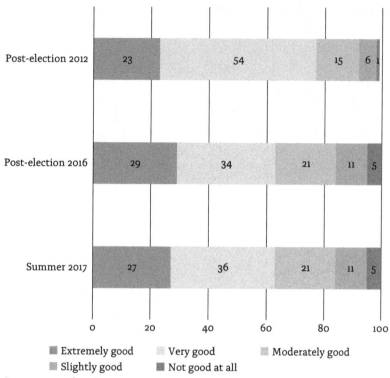

Source: 2012 and 2016–2017 Latino Immigrant National Election Studies.

remaining in the United States or repatriating, these attitude breakdowns also do not suggest a "softer" exit in the form of a withdrawal
from U.S. society.

Two other items on the LINES questionnaire tapped into general
feelings toward the country: "When you see the American flag flying,
how do you feel?" And, "In general, how do you feel about the United
States?" These questions were part of the post-election LINES survey
in 2012 and the two survey waves conducted after the 2016 election.
Responses are given in figures 4.6 and 4.7. In both cases, we see that in
the post-election transition period and the summer of 2017, feelings
toward the flag and the country remained fairly similar to what was
measured in 2012. Regarding attitudes toward the flag (figure 4.6),
immigrants were slightly more prone in 2016 and 2017 to feel less

Figure 4.7 *"In General, How Do You Feel About the United States?": U.S.-Centric Patriotism Among Latino Immigrants, 2012 and 2016–2017*

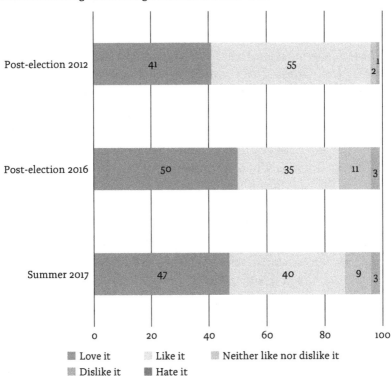

Source: 2012 and 2016–2017 Latino Immigrant National Election Studies.

than "extremely good" or "very good" compared to 2012. But the number expressing the most positive feelings actually rose slightly— from 23 percent in 2012 to 29 percent in the transition period following the 2016 election and 27 percent the following summer.

For the item on feelings toward the United States overall, the distributions of responses in the aggregate were largely stable from 2012 to 2017. As with the earlier figure, Latino immigrants in 2016 and 2017 were somewhat more inclined to report "loving" the United States compared to 2012. In all three survey periods, no respondents indicated that they "hated" America, and the percentage that "disliked" the country was vanishingly low—never more than 3 percent. This pattern contrasts with the trends in evaluations of American government institutions that were modeled in the previous chapter.

Clearly, a loss of faith in the trustworthiness and integrity of officials in the federal government under the Trump administration is not paired with more expansive hostility toward the country as a whole and its primary symbol, the flag.

At the individual level, the item on trust and feelings toward the country was regressed on the different civic stress measures, using the same analytical setup employed to model changes in repatriation planning. For the questions on feelings about the United States and the American flag, attitudes were about as stable as evaluations of the U.S. government from the presidential transition period to the summer of 2017. Changes in these feelings, however, were not linked in any significant way to pessimism about the direction of the country, anger or anxiety concerning Trump, or concerns about deportations or family finances. This interpretation holds even when the different civic stress items are allowed to interact with an immigrant's civic status, the number of years he or she had lived in the country, the policy disposition toward immigrants within the respondent's state of residence, and whether or not the respondent was Mexican-origin. Immigrants who were not naturalized citizens, were relative newcomers to the United States, resided in an unwelcoming state, or had emigrated from Mexico reacted to civic stresses in the same way, insofar as attitudes toward the nation and its flag were concerned. These generally positive feelings were resilient across the board.

The item on interpersonal trust was quite resilient as well amid civic stresses. As was the case with plans to remain in the United States or repatriate, we find that concerns about the possible deportation of family members or friends led to a decline in trust during the presidential transition period. But this effect only approached statistical significance ($p = .17$); it was not substantively noteworthy, and there is no evidence that deportation worries had a comparable impact on interpersonal trust in the summer of 2017. Furthermore, the effects of the other civic stress items on trust were even weaker. Nor did the effects of these items on interpersonal trust vary significantly in either survey period based on civic status, time spent in the United States, whether the respondent lived in a welcoming or unwelcoming state, or Mexican- versus non-Mexican-origin.

In moments of political frustration or anxiety, residents of the United States—immigrants and the native-born alike—may blurt out a desire to flee the country. It is one thing to blow off steam, however, and another to make plans to leave. For Latino immigrants, widespread misgivings about the direction of the country under Trump and the well-being of their friends and family led to doubts about the trustworthiness and soundness of American governing institutions, but not to a distancing from U.S. society or its symbols. The sense that the country is moving in the wrong direction was not mirrored in a detachment from the country itself. There is no evidence for either "hard" or "soft" exiting among Latinos immigrants. Holding fast in the face of challenging headwinds bodes well for political engagement—the topic we turn to next.

RAISING VOICES IN RESPONSE TO CIVIC STRESS   5

HOW MANY DECIBELS?

On April 10, 2006, Isabel Garcia, an eighteen-year-old high school student in Frankfort, Indiana, got up early to carpool to Indianapolis with nine other Latino students to take part in protest marches that were part of the "National Day of Action for Immigrant Justice."[1] The group had originally planned to charter buses to take them and other activists from rural north-central Indiana to the state capital that morning, but these initial plans fell through. Isabel recalled many years later that, while driving south on Interstate 65 for about an hour to reach Indianapolis, she and her friends listened to Ricardo Arjona's "Mojado" on an almost continuous loop. This Latin Grammy Award–nominated song from 2005 tells the story of a migrant who crossed the border without papers, bringing only a few personal possessions, dreaming of a better life in the United States, and feeling sad and anxious but trusting in divine guidance and protection. The young protesters considered this their theme music for the day. "Why do I need permission," she remembered the artist singing, "if God already gave me permission?"

Such lyrics spoke to the migration story of Isabel and her family. Originally from a small village in the Mexican state of Michoacán, she, her parents, and two younger siblings came to the United States without entry papers in 1994. Floating on a large truck tire, the family crossed the Rio Grande with the assistance of a coyote and traveled directly to Frankfort, where one of Isabel's uncles had previously settled and there was a great deal of demand for immigrant labor.[2] Shortly thereafter, the U.S. Congress added a special provision to the Immigration and Nationality Act that permitted undocumented immigrants to gain legal permanency and eventually citizenship on the basis of kinship relationships or job skills. Isabel and her family took advantage of this provision, which was in force for only a few years.[3] In 1995, Isabel received a green card, and some years later she became an American citizen.

This change in her civic status notwithstanding, she reported having a hard time in middle school, recalling frequent doubts about whether she was really accepted by her classmates and whether she truly belonged. The other members of Isabel's family carried around similar doubts, but they participated in activities of the local Catholic parish that fostered a sense of security and community, as well as a sense of justifiable indignation. Isabel reported first hearing about the National Day of Action for Immigrant Justice through contacts at her church.

As the carpoolers approached Indianapolis, traffic slowed to a snail's pace; activists were pouring in from all directions. Police officials estimated that 20,000 people participated in a half-mile march through the city center to show their support for immigrants.[4] In over sixty other U.S. cities, comparable demonstrations took place that day. And this was hardly the only day for direct action on immigration. Throughout the country between February and June 2006, news outlets reported 268 protest events on behalf of immigrants.[5] In total, an estimated 3.7 million to 5.0 million people took to the streets, a level of engagement that far surpassed the number of activists who turned out for the 1963 March on Washington for Jobs and Freedom, the 1969 marches to end the Vietnam War, and the 1886 Chicago Haymarket protest.[6]

The central rallying call for immigrant rights activists in 2006 was opposition to a measure that the U.S. House of Representatives had passed in late 2005, H.R. 4437, the Border Protection, Anti-terrorism, and Illegal Immigration Control Act. More commonly known as the Sensenbrenner Bill, in recognition of its chief sponsor, Representative Jim Sensenbrenner, Republican from Wisconsin, this legislation would have made a lack of residency authorization for immigrants a felony with a mandatory prison sentence. In a separate provision, anyone assisting undocumented immigrants by, say, taking them to a doctor would risk criminal prosecution as well. The bill also called for more surveillance along the southern border with Mexico and increased immigration enforcement within the interior of the United States.

The possibility that these harsh and unprecedented sanctions against immigrants and their supporters might be signed into law sparked immediate pushback. Chris Zepeda-Millán reports that a wide array of immigrant-friendly organizations—religious congregations, Latino small-business owners, neighborhood clubs for emigrants from particular cities or regions, and ethnic media networks, among others—subsidized and sustained grassroots protest activities throughout the spring. "We all chipped-in. . . . I spent more than $1,000 on the event," said the owner of a Mexican restaurant in Florida when asked about his involvement in a particular demonstration. "All my friends around here gave money."[7]

Immigrant rights activists that spring were successful in their most immediate goal. When the Sensenbrenner Bill was sent to the Republican-controlled Senate, a cloture vote to end a filibuster failed, which effectively stopped any further legislative action on the bill. However, the protests did not bring about the activists' ultimate goal—comprehensive immigration policy reform with a pathway to citizenship for immigrants without papers. Rather, in the aftermath of the 2006 demonstrations, pro-immigrant and anti-immigrant positions among policymakers in Washington further hardened, thus making congressional compromises across the partisan aisle on immigration all but impossible.

Fast-forward several years: even though no anti-immigrant measures comparable to those in the Sensenbrenner Bill have made it through the House of Representatives since 2005, unilateral actions taken by the White House under President Trump, starting in 2017, have restricted the rights of immigrants in ways that in some respects go beyond what Sensenbrenner called for. These executive actions have been discussed in earlier chapters, as have the disappointments, anxieties, and anger that many immigrants felt in the first year of the Trump administration. In this chapter, we consider whether these feelings prompted foreign-born Latinos to raise their voices again, and if so, how loudly.

To anticipate our findings, the LINES panel survey points to such dynamics: the number of "decibels" of political voice among Latino immigrants in the first year of the Trump administration did not quite match the 2006 mobilization, but it still rose. Much has been written about the remarkable protest demonstrations for women's rights, racial justice, and environmental protection following the 2016 election. And in the more conventional electoral arena, the turnout rate in the 2018 midterm elections was equally remarkable—just over 50 percent of the voting-eligible population turned out, the highest level of involvement in a midterm contest since the early 1900s. In this chapter, we show that foreign-born Latinos were a key part of this participatory outpouring: immigrant voices have complemented those that have been raised from other quarters of American society.

The Roots of Immigrant Participation

In any democracy, the people who take part in politics through voting, attending community issue forums, contacting government officials, engaging in street protests, or any other activities are invariably a subset of the total adult population. Everyone may have a right to participate in some fashion, but only a portion of the public actually turns out. Why some people are involved in political activities while others abstain tells us much about the quality of democratic representation. Individuals who raise their voice in politics stand a chance of influencing government policies and practices. Those who do not may well be ignored and forgotten whenever policymakers meet.

When investigating political participation, researchers commonly take as a starting premise that decisions on whether or not to take part stem from informal calculations about "costs" and "benefits." People who follow public affairs and get some amount of enjoyment from keeping on top of the news, who see themselves as part of larger social groups with distinctive interests, or who have strong preferences on policy issues are naturally drawn into political activities. This is certainly a core pillar of representative democracy—individuals who feel strongly about politics and policies are expected to act on their interests. Engagement in politics, however, can be costly in terms of time and financial resources and may incur other expenses as well. People with less wherewithal to pay these costs—for instance, those of more modest means, with limited education, or with fewer life experiences—might find it hard to engage even if they wish to do so. The social and political networks in which a person is enmeshed also matter. An individual's cost-benefit calculations are affected when a friend, colleague, or political canvasser asks him or her to participate in a political event or simply turn out to vote. Such interpersonal contacts can reinforce the subjectively felt benefits of involvement while simultaneously reducing the costs. In their classic *Voice and Equality*, Sidney Verba, Kay Lehman Schlozman, and Henry Brady bundle these considerations together in the pithy observation that people do not become active in politics "because they can't; because they don't want to; or because nobody asked."[8]

Viewing the decision to participate in politics as a function of implicit costs and benefits makes a good deal of intuitive sense. For Latino immigrants, taking an active interest in U.S. politics could well correlate with various kinds of involvement, as it does within the general population. Other personal motivating factors would include the politically relevant social identities that one might adopt while becoming acculturated into American civic life, one's policy preferences, and confidence that one can figure out the intricacies of politics in the United States. This last factor is conventionally labeled "personal political efficacy"—a sense that politics and government are not too complicated to understand.

With respect to social identifications, the most important would be partisanship. Recent research on immigrant partisanship suggests that foreign-born Latinos do not consider themselves members of a party to the same degree as U.S.-born Americans, owing to a general lack of socialization as children into the party system. However, a substantial number of Latino immigrants are nevertheless open to identifying as a partisan, with the overwhelming number siding with the Democrats. One study, for example, finds that during the 2012 campaign cycle levels of identification with the Democratic Party among Latino immigrants nearly matched that of U.S.-born Latinos (45 versus 48 percent, respectively). Another study reports that this degree of similarity between foreign- and U.S.-born Latinos was not unique to the political environment in 2012. In the 2006 midterm elections and 2008 presidential contest, immigrants from Mexico were just as open to identifying as Democrats as Latinos who were born and raised in the United States. In all of these election cycles, the number of immigrants considering themselves Republican was low, but not vanishingly low—between

5 and 10 percent.[9] In principle, partisan identities such as these could spark involvement in a wide range of political activities. As Nancy Rosenblum writes in her "appreciation" of parties and partisanship, "Partisans spend more, not less time attending to politics. They have more hooks for taking in new information. . . . Partisans are more motivated, take more interest in electoral competition, and care more about who wins."[10]

Partisanship, however, is not the only relevant social identity that might prompt immigrant engagement in politics. As Latin America–born immigrants become more acquainted with U.S. politics and society, many adopt a pan-ethnic identification—a belief that one is a Latino or Hispanic in addition to being, say, a Guatemalan, Colombian, or Cuban. Such pan-ethnic orientations have been linked to various modes of political involvement.[11] Seeing oneself as part of a larger ethnic group can promote a sense of solidarity and draw attention to the need for collective political action. Taking strong stances on key public policy issues that disproportionately affect ethnic communities may also motivate immigrants to become involved. Policies concerning naturalization and deportation would certainly be the most salient in this regard.

Pre-migration experiences in politics also undoubtedly shape patterns of involvement in American civic life. Although each Latin American country has a distinctive form of government, none of which directly matches that of the United States, the experience of taking part in politics prior to emigrating may spur continued involvement after settlement. The appendix figure for this chapter (figure 5.A1) shows the distribution of these various items in the summer of 2017, some months after Donald Trump entered the White House and began implementing his agenda. Collectively, these survey indicators speak to the "they don't want to" dimension in the (non)participation calculus of Verba and his colleagues. Overall, we observe considerable variability in these motivational items—variations that could determine who is or is not involved.

The "they can't" part of the (non)participation calculus refers to resources that might otherwise help "pay" for the implicit costs of involvement. Within the general public, socioeconomic status is commonly held up as a key factor—a person's education level, level of affluence, and age, among other demographic traits. All things equal, it is typically the case that better-educated individuals who are older and wealthier participate more in politics. Being more exposed to formal education, possessing more disposable income, and being able to draw upon a wealth of life experiences are all said to enlarge one's capacity to engage in public affairs. Race and gender are also frequently linked to involvement of one kind or another. Such socioeconomic factors do not always prompt participation by the foreign-born population, however, in the same ways as they do with the general public. Being educated in the school system of another country, for example, may not have the same "payoff" in terms of imparting politically relevant resources for political activity in the U.S. context. And older immigrants may be less rather than more inclined to participate. Carole Uhlaner and her colleagues suggest that younger immigrants tend to be more open to trying out new behaviors after settling in the United States, including participation in political activities.[12]

The length of time an immigrant has resided in the United States can also be considered a potentially important resource that leads to participation. Exposure to American politics over time could breed familiarity with U.S. democratic norms, thereby allowing immigrants to better afford the implicit costs of involvement. Familiarity with English could also boost resources for involvement, inasmuch as national dialogues concerning campaigns and issues, even absent an "official" U.S. language, are conducted largely in English. Citizenship is certainly a key resource within this population as well. Immigrants who are not naturalized citizens are formally blocked from participation in federal elections—a formal administrative barrier that perfectly captures the "they can't" element of the (non) participation calculus of Verba and his colleagues. Such a barrier could indirectly depress involvement in other kinds of political involvement as well.[13]

With respect to the "nobody asked" part of this calculus, our attention is easily drawn to the kinds of social networking and people-to-people contacting that may pull immigrants into American political life. In his classic work on social capital, Robert Putnam, echoing Alexis de Tocqueville, highlights these sorts of interpersonal connections as the foundation upon which American democracy is built.[14] Individuals who are well networked within their community

are explicitly or implicitly "asked" to take part in politics when opportunities present themselves. Involvement is not as burdensome or
costly for them, and the benefits of involvement may stand out in
greater relief in comparison to any such benefits that might accrue
to those who are less established in their local community.

For immigrants, involvement in religious activities, putting down
roots within a particular neighborhood, and contacts with political
activists during election campaigns might all serve to make American
politics more approachable. These networks may reduce the costliness
of political information and sharpen one's politically relevant identities and interests. Other important resources are the "hometown"
clubs and social service organizations for immigrants that have
been established in many locations around the United States. These
neighborhood groups honor and support cities or regions in migrant-
sending countries. For example, a number of Salvadoran hometown
associations were established in response to the devastation caused by
Hurricane Mitch in 1998. Other associations celebrate cultural events
in the sending country.[15] Because these organizations connect immigrants within their local communities, they may serve as important
sources of social capital. Although hometown associate events would
be oriented toward the country of origin, such transnational clubs
may clarify for participants the policies that affect immigrants
within the United States. In this sense, they could add to the foundation for immigrant engagement.

Thinking of immigrants' involvement in politics as a function of
costs and benefits leads us to focus on the variations in their interests and collective group identities that animate participation, the
resources that bolster their capacity to become active, and person-
to-person mobilizing networks. As shown in figure 5.A1, many
foreign-born Latinos in the summer of 2017 reported following
politics regularly, expressed strong policy interests, felt confident
that they could understand politics, saw themselves as part of a
larger ethnic or partisan group in the United States, and had experience voting in an election prior to emigrating. Many others, however,
were not so inclined to participate. Moreover, a substantial number
of foreign-born Latinos lack the kinds of resources that could steer
them toward engagement. The majority, for instance, are not citizens, and most speak Spanish in their everyday lives. Levels of formal

education also tend to be lower among foreign-born Latinos, as does family income. Additionally, much prior research on immigrants and the U.S. party system faults the parties for lacking long-term strategies to mobilize the foreign-born population.[16] Because both Democrats and Republicans tend to fixate on short-term mobilization goals in an election, they contact their most reliable supporters, the vast majority of whom would not be foreign-born.

In many Latino communities, church leaders are quite prominent, and most foreign-born Latinos say that religion is an important part of their lives.[17] This does not necessarily equate, however, to regular involvement in church activities. In the LINES survey, fewer than one out of three foreign-born Latinos reported attending religious services each week. Even fewer—approximately one out of ten—were active in a hometown club for immigrants. All of this is to say that for a large portion of the contemporary Latin America–born population in the United States, the benefits of taking part in politics might be overshadowed by the costs.

The preceding chapters showed that Latino immigrants generally hold positive views of Americans and U.S. society, even if there has been a decline in faith in governing institutions under President Trump. The fact that many are undermotivated, underresourced, or undermobilized, however, could imply that the voices they raise in this era of rising pressures and threats are rather muted. Before jumping to this conclusion, we should take into account another dimension of political action—the emotional underpinnings of involvement. Political observers have long recognized that emotional reactions to leaders, policies, and one's immediate living conditions can prompt engagement. To refer again to James Madison and his classic *Federalist 10*, political activity in any free society is necessarily a product of "some common impulse of passion, or of interest." In this spirit, the calculus of (non)participation put forth by Verba, Schlozman, and Brady—"they don't care," "they can't," or "nobody asked"—could be fruitfully enriched to include "passions have not yet been sufficiently aroused."

In earlier chapters, we have seen that disappointment with the direction of the country, feelings of fear and anger toward Donald Trump, concerns about the deportation of friends or family members, and worries about the financial well-being of one's family were certainly aroused for most of the immigrants in the LINES survey. What effects do these concerns and fears have on immigrants' political engagement? As we discussed in chapter 2, psychologists generally agree that anger prompts action—an angry person can be a true force to reckon with. Individuals feeling disappointment or fear may become more cautious and may duck and cover when threats are looming. This would be a natural initial response. These various negative emotions, however, tend to be closely related. Anger can overlap with fear, as is certainly the case when immigrants size up Donald Trump. Such an overlap suggests that when a person is fearful or pessimistic, he or she may also become aroused at some juncture to target the source of the perceived threats.

For Isabel Garcia and her friends as they drove south on Interstate 65 toward Indianapolis to take part in the National Day of Action for Immigrant Justice in April 2006, these emotions—righteous indignation, fear, and sadness—were deeply felt, commingled, and heartrending. In the following section, we show that similar dynamics were at work among foreign-born Latinos nationwide after the 2016 election, and that these feelings helped to spur comparable political engagement.

Analysis and Findings

Any reflections on political engagement after the inauguration of President Trump would have to begin with the massive and remarkable women's marches that commenced on January 21, 2017. An estimated 3.3 million to 4.6 million activists turned out to protest the new administration, the largest political demonstration by far on a single day in American history. There is much to learn about the roots of this mobilization, though the most immediate cause is obvious. Throughout his business career and as a candidate for president, Donald Trump became embroiled in a number of sexual harassment lawsuits. He also had a long record of misogynistic statements, the most notable being his extremely offensive banter with television host Billy Bush in 2005, a recording of which surfaced at the height of the 2016 campaign. With Trump as president, women's rights activists feared the worst and banded together in solidarity.

Figure 5.1 *Count of Protest Events by Year and Issue Area, 2017–2019*

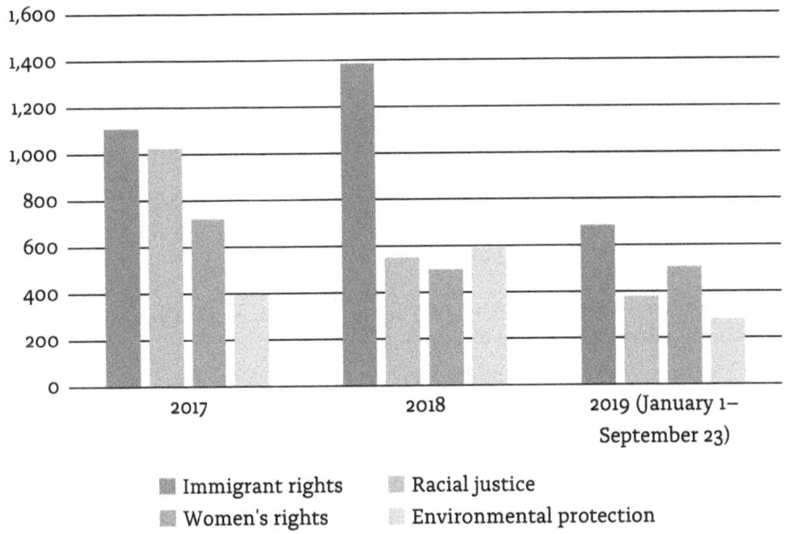

Legend:
- Immigrant rights
- Racial justice
- Women's rights
- Environmental protection

Source: Count Love, https://countlove.org/.
Note: Data on protest events were gathered through a daily computational tally of reports from local newspaper and television sites.

Coinciding with these marches, but attracting much less media attention, were protests for racial justice, environmental protection, and immigrant rights. These protests did not draw nearly as many participants, but the outpouring was nevertheless striking. Figure 5.1 presents an estimated count of the number of protest events in each of these issue areas, aggregated by year. For 2019, the tally extends through the summer, ending on September 23. We should stress that these numbers are not exact. Tallies of demonstration events are based on published newspaper and television accounts, monitored on a daily basis by "web-crawling" software. If, say, twenty individuals in upstate Pennsylvania turned out to protest police discrimination within the minority community, the web crawler would pick this up based on local reporting newsfeeds.[18]

We find in this figure that in 2017 and continuing into 2019, a substantial number of immigrant rights protest demonstrations were staged: 1,108 in 2017, 1,385 in 2018, and 684 in the winter, spring, and summer of 2019. These tallies are impressive and actually

Figure 5.2 *Involvement of Latino Immigrants in Rallies, Protests, and Demonstrations, 2006, 2012, 2016–2017*

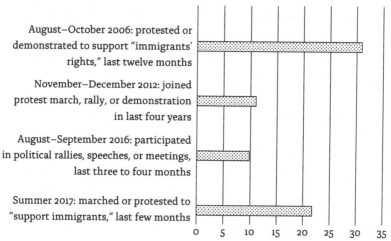

Source: Pew Hispanic Center, "Data and Resources," https://www.pewresearch.org/hispanic/data-and-resources/; 2012 and 2016–2017 Latino Immigrant National Election Studies.

outnumber demonstrations on behalf of women's rights, environmental protection, and racial justice. Turnout estimates for immigrant rights protests, however, are far lower than those for women's rights and many of the other demonstrations—perhaps not surprisingly, since immigrants are still a relatively small fraction of the U.S. population. Consequently, however, rallies for immigrant rights have not been as vivid in the public consciousness as in the spring of 2006, when many millions of activists turned out in very visible, large rallies in major cities. Yet there is no doubt that immigrants and their allies have been raising their political voices since the 2016 election.

Surveys of Latino immigrants over time further demonstrate these dynamics. In a poll conducted by the Pew Hispanic Center in 2006, nearly one out of three foreign-born Latinos indicated that they had taken part in a protest demonstration to support immigrant rights over the last twelve months (figure 5.2). This notably high incidence of engagement comports with aggregate estimates of crowd sizes at marches and demonstrations that year. Six years later, respondents to the 2012 Latino Immigrant National Election Study were asked if they had participated in a protest, march, rally, or demonstration over the last four years. At that point, the wave of immigrant rights protests had clearly subsided. Approximately one-tenth of the survey respondents in this study indicated that they had taken to the streets. This was the case as well in 2016; just under 10 percent stated then that they had participated in political rallies, listened to speeches, or gone to meetings over the last few months. But come the summer of 2017, we see a considerable uptick in marches and protest activism among Latino immigrants. Although the level of involvement did not match what was found in the 2006 Pew survey, it came close. Over one out of five immigrants in the third wave of the LINES survey (summer of 2017) reported turning out to take part in protests—another impressive showing that fits with the counts of protest events displayed in figure 5.1. This suggests that Latino immigrants responded to the new and serious civic stresses following the 2016 election by raising their voices in direct action.

We can elaborate on this interpretation through regression modeling. What were the main drivers of participation in protest demonstrations? As a first step, turnout at an immigrant rights demonstration or march in 2017 was regressed on a very wide range of survey items that collectively capture the cost-benefit dimensions of involvement: general interest in politics; partisan identification; identification as "Latino" or "Hispanic"; personal political efficacy; stance on U.S. immigration policy; experience voting in an election prior to emigrating to the United States; participation in political rallies, speeches, or meetings during the fall 2016 campaign; level of formal education; family income; gender; age; number of years spent in the United States; language use at home; civic status (naturalized citizen, green-card-holder, or noncitizen without a green card); country of origin (Mexico versus another country); involvement in local "hometown" associations; amount of remittances sent to family and friends in the country of origin; number of family and friends in the country of origin; marital status; attendance at religious services; homeownership; the policy disposition toward immigrants in respondent's state of residence; and contact with political activists during the 2016 campaign.

Each of these items was entered on its own into a bivariate logistic regression model in order to gauge the most direct (that is, "uncontrolled") impact of a particular variable on protest involvement. Then all predictors were entered simultaneously into an expansive summary regression model. Both approaches yielded the same results: for the most part, participation in a march or protest for immigrant rights was *not* a function of these many items. The many nonfindings in the bivariate and multivariate regressions further tell us that involvement in this most unconventional form of political activity is not well explained by conventional cost-benefit factors. The only predictor that attained statistical significance in a bivariate or multivariate regression model was the age of the respondent.

In keeping with earlier work, we find that younger immigrants were more apt to have turned out to protest. The chart in figure 5.3 portrays this relationship. After controlling for all of the survey items previously discussed, the multivariate regression model predicts that for immigrants who were twenty-five years old, the probability of taking part in a protest event was .32. That is to say, about one in three young adults responding to our surveys indicated they had joined a protest. Holding all else constant, this predicted probability drops to .15 for immigrants who were fifty-five. As with the 2006 immigrant rights protests, it appears that younger immigrants were the principal catalysts of these kinds of civic engagement.

We thus turn our attention to the LINES items from the summer of 2017 that tap into discontent and emotional arousal: a belief that the United States is on the "wrong track"; feelings of anger, fear, or both toward President Trump; worries that a friend or family member will face deportation; and concerns about family finances. After taking into account the many predictors cited earlier, each of these items was entered one by one into the multivariate regression model. Figure 5.4 displays the results. As we would expect, each of these predictors is positively linked to protest activism. Two stand out as particularly relevant and statistically significant:

- The predicted probability of turning out for a protest rally is nearly *ten points higher* for immigrants who reported both anger and fear toward Trump than for immigrants who expressed neither anger

Figure 5.3 *Predicted Probability of Latino Immigrants' Participation in a March or Protest to Support Immigrants in the First Year of the Trump Administration, by Age*

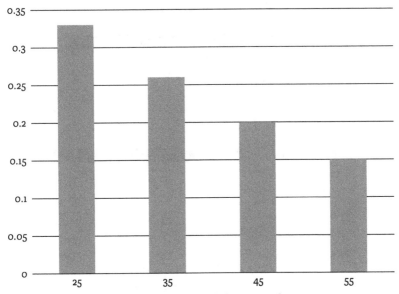

Source: 2016–2017 Latino Immigrant National Election Study.
Note: The relationship between age and participation is statistically significant (*p* < .01). Controls are in place for involvement in political meetings, rallies, and dinners before the 2016 election; membership in a hometown association for immigrants; political mobilization during the 2016 campaign; general interest in politics; party identification; personal political efficacy; preferences concerning immigration policy reform; identification as "Latino" or "Hispanic"; civic status; length of time living in the United States; pre-migration participation in elections; transnational social networks; language use at home; gender; education level; family income; attendance at religious services; marital status; homeownership; policy disposition toward immigrants in one's state of residence; and country of origin (Mexican-born versus emigration from another Latin American country). None of these controls is statistically significant in the logistic regression model.

nor fear. In the former group, the regression model predicts a probability of protesting of .24. This drops to .15 in the latter group, all other factors equal.

- For immigrants who were extremely concerned that a friend or family member would be deported, the predicted probability of attending a demonstration is over *ten points higher* compared to those with no such concerns (.25 versus .14).

Figure 5.4 *Impact of Civic Stress on Latino Immigrants' Involvement in a March or Protest to Support Immigrants in the First Year of the Trump Administration*

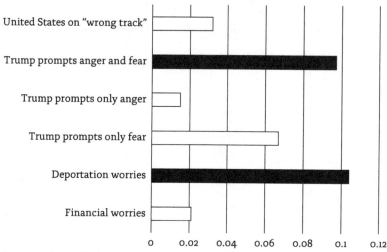

Source: 2016–2017 Latino Immigrant National Election Study.

Note: The bars show impacts on involvement as a given type of civic stress increases from its lowest to highest value. Light gray shading indicates statistical significance at the .10 level; solid black bars are significant at the .05 level. Civic stresses as measured in the third wave were used to predict participation. When calculating these impacts, we controlled for a respondent's involvement in rallies and other expressive political events before the 2016 election; general interest in politics; party identification; personal political efficacy; preference on immigration policy reform; civic status; length of time living in the United States; transnational social networks; pre-migration involvement in elections; language use at home; gender; age; education level; family income; attendance at religious services; marital status; homeownership; policy disposition toward immigrants in one's state of residence; and country of origin (Mexican-born versus emigration from another Latin American country).

Expanding on these findings, it is reasonable to conclude that the thousands of immigrant rights protest events that have been staged since the 2016 elections have been animated, at least in part, by deeply negative emotional reactions to the new president and not-unreasonable concerns that friends or loved ones are at risk. The "personal" has very much been political. It is further worth noting that the effects of civic stress on protest activism have not varied depending on whether or not the respondent was a natural-ized citizen, the respondent's length of stay in the United States, the policy disposition toward immigrants in the state where the respondent resides, or whether or not the respondent was Mexican-origin.[19] When distressed, LINES respondents who were less vulnerable and better established in the United States demonstrated to the same extent as more vulnerable immigrants.

The many activists attending these protests have clearly not sought incremental changes in public policy. Speakers at rallies and demonstrations typically call for far-reaching reforms, including an immediate pathway to citizenship for undocumented immigrants, the demilitarization of the U.S.-Mexico border, stepped-up public services for the foreign-born, dramatically larger budgets for refugee support and resettlement, and the abolition of the U.S. Immigration and Customs Enforcement Agency, among other demands.

Such expressions of political voice and solidarity are no doubt cathartic for activists and serve to bring greater visibility to the issues surrounding the plight of undocumented migrants in the United States. But are protest activities of this sort displacing more conventional forms of voice-raising for immigrants? To be sure, in any democracy, protest movements can help shape governing agendas. But much constructive work in a democracy also takes place in less confrontational settings, where demands are more measured—for example, in neighborhood meetings to address common concerns, or through direct contacts with government officials. If rallying for their rights pulls immigrants away from these more common kinds of political activities, their trajectory of democratic incorporation could suffer.

Is this happening? Three LINES items on conventional political involvement allow us to examine this question. In the initial pre-election survey in 2016 and again in the summer of 2017, immigrants indicated whether over the last few months they had attended a meeting about an issue facing their community or schools; worked with others to deal with some issue facing the community; or contacted a government official either in a personal visit or by telephone, letter, or email to express their views. The chart in figure 5.5 shows the distributions for these items in each survey wave. A key pattern emerges here: for all three forms of participation, we find an increase in involvement over time. In August and September 2016, 25 percent of LINES respondents indicated that they had recently attended a community meeting, 19 percent had engaged in local

Figure 5.5 *Political Involvement of Latino Immigrants, 2016–2017*

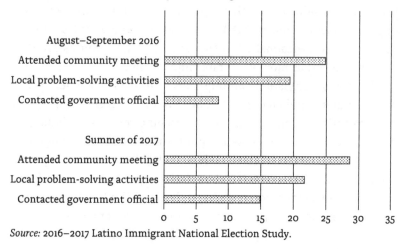

Source: 2016–2017 Latino Immigrant National Election Study.

Figure 5.6 *Correlation Between Latino Immigrants' Protest Activism and Conventional Political Participation, 2017*

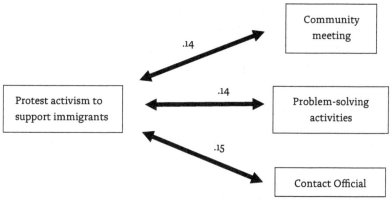

Source: 2016–2017 Latino Immigrant National Election Study.
Note: These correlations are all highly significant ($p < .01$).

problem-solving activities, and 8 percent had contacted a government official in the recent past. Come the summer of 2017, these figures rose to 29, 22, and 15 percent, respectively. It appears that as immigrants became more engaged in protest activities, there was a concurrent uptick in more ordinary types of involvement as well.

The findings presented in figure 5.6 make this point more directly. Attending an immigrant rights protest is positively—not

Figure 5.7 *Effect of Latino Immigrants' Participation in Immigrant Rights Protests on Their Conventional Participation: Predicted Probabilities*

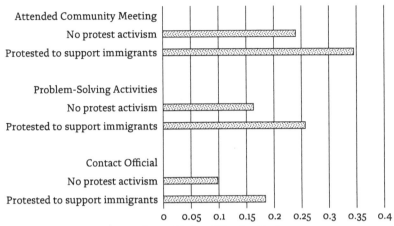

Attended Community Meeting
No protest activism
Protested to support immigrants

Problem-Solving Activities
No protest activism
Protested to support immigrants

Contact Official
No protest activism
Protested to support immigrants

0   0.05   0.1   0.15   0.2   0.25   0.3   0.35   0.4

Source: 2016–2017 Latino Immigrant National Election Study.

Note: Predicted probabilities were calculated based on logistic regression models, with controls in place for political involvement before the 2016 election; general interest in politics; party identification; personal political efficacy; preference on immigration policy reform; civic status; length of time living in the United States; transnational social networks; pre-migration involvement in elections; language use at home; age; gender; education level; family income; attendance at religious services; marital status; homeownership; policy disposition toward immigrants in respondent's state of residence; country of origin (Mexican-born versus emigration from another Latin American country); beliefs about the direction of the country; emotional reactions to President Trump; worries that a friend or family member may be deported; and concerns about family finances. The positive relationship between protest activism and each form of conventional participation is highly significant ($p < .01$).

negatively—correlated with these three other participation measures. Of course, these correlations are far from perfect. Yet the fact that there are significant positive connections across these distinct modes of involvement suggests that seemingly antisystemic protest mobilization is in fact not so "antisystemic." Rather, for Latino immigrants, protest involvement and conventional participation may be mutually reinforcing.

A final set of results for this chapter illustrates this relationship. Figure 5.7 presents the predicted probabilities of respondents attending community meetings, engaging in problem-solving activities, and contacting government officials in 2017, broken down by whether or not the respondent was involved in protest activism that year. These probabilities are calculated based on logistic regression models, where controls are in place for all of the many motivational, resource, and mobilization variables mentioned earlier plus the items on civic stresses. After taking into account these many factors, it is clear that involvement in immigrant rights demonstrations has a fairly pronounced positive effect on the three conventional participation items. The same immigrants who take to the streets to demand sweeping changes in government policy might in the following week also attend a meeting of the local school board or email a state representative to voice concerns.

Conclusion

The rise of contentious mass protest movements in Western democracies over the last several generations has often been interpreted as a sign of deep-seated political or social alienation, a sense of disaffection that is so severe that it cannot be channeled effectively through established conduits of representation. When such direct action in the streets persists and spreads, commentators have frequently warned that the moral authority of a political system is being called into question. For many observers, the social movement demonstrations of the 1960s and '70s sent such a signal.[20]

The story line of this chapter presents a very different portrait of marches, rallies, and other direct-action mobilizations within immigrant communities. The findings complement those in the preceding two chapters. The immigrants who took part in the LINES survey harbored well-founded concerns about their well-being and the well-being of the country. These concerns have made them more skeptical about U.S. governing institutions. Yet there remains an abiding faith in American society.

Involvement in street demonstrations can be taken as an additional sign of faith. Isabel Garcia and her friends devoted much time and energy to protest activism in 2006 because they believed that they had a legitimate right to raise their voices and be heard. In 2017, we find no evidence that social and economic marginalization, estrangement from political parties, or a lack of personal political efficacy shaped the immigrant rights movement. Protests were instead an understandable manifestation of immigrants' fear and anger. Far from turning them en masse against the political system, protesting may well reinforce the habits of everyday democratic political engagement.

Figure 5.A1 *Items to Capture Latino Immigrants' Motivations to Take Part in Politics, Summer of 2017*

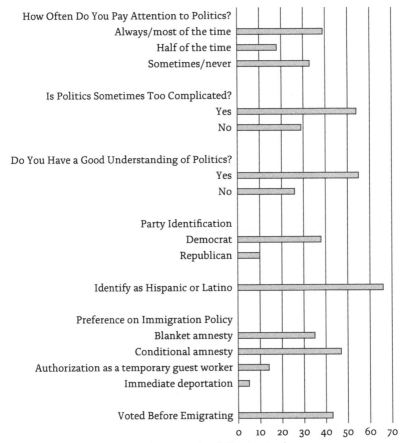

Source: 2016–2017 Latino Immigrant National Election Study.

CONCLUSION   6

The 2018 midterm elections were remarkable in many respects. The forty-one seats that the Democratic Party gained in the House of Representatives returned the party to majority status by a sizable margin. To find a comparable shift in the partisan balance of the House of Representatives, we would have to look back to the 1974 midterm election cycle, when the Republican Party was in free fall following the Watergate scandal and the resignation of President Richard Nixon. The 2018 midterm elections were also noteworthy for the prodigious efforts of social movement leaders and partisan officials—especially Democratic Party officials—to recruit women to run for office. As a consequence, the 116th Congress (2019–2021) has the largest class of female lawmakers ever. The two chambers of Congress also became more racially and ethnically diverse. In the 2019–2020 congressional term, nearly one out of four lawmakers was a member of a minority group (African American, Latino, Asian American, or Native American). As late as 2008, the percentage of minority lawmakers was only half that size. And as mentioned in the previous chapter, the voter turnout rate in 2018 was astounding. Approximately 50 percent of all eligible voters took part, the highest level for a midterm election in over a century. Clearly, if the 2016 presidential election cycle constituted an earthquake in American party politics, it was followed by an equally consequential after-shock in the 2018 midterms.

Perhaps the most relevant feature of these midterms for the themes of this book was the diversity of the electorate, a trajectory match-ing the increasing diversity among congressional representatives.

Figure 6.1 *Racial and Ethnic Composition of Midterm Electorates, 2002–2018*

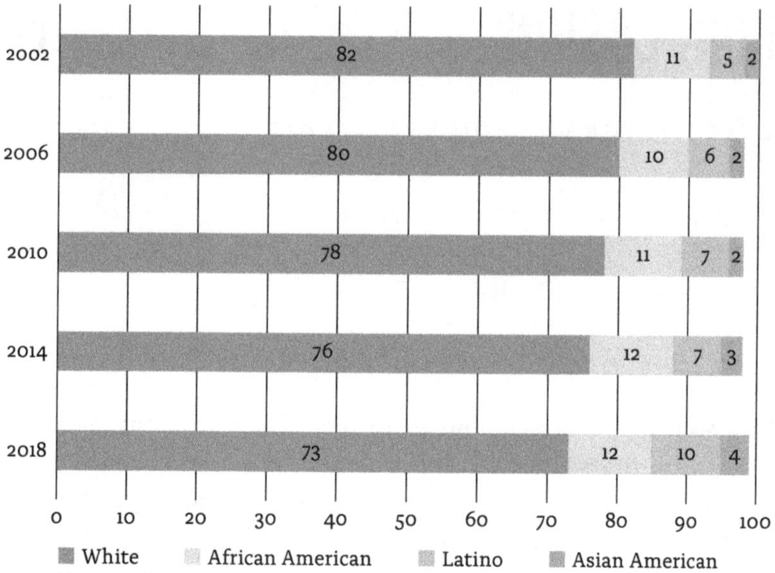

Year	White	African American	Latino	Asian American
2002	82	11	5	2
2006	80	10	6	2
2010	78	11	7	2
2014	76	12	7	3
2018	73	12	10	4

■ White   African American   ▒ Latino   ■ Asian American

Source: Krogstad, Noe-Bustamante, and Flores 2019.

The sizable uptick in participation that year was observable across all racial and ethnic groups. The midterm electorate of 2018 was more ethnically and racially diverse than just four years earlier (as shown in figure 6.1), and it was considerably more diverse than at the turn of the twenty-first century. In addition, data from the 2018 American Community Survey suggests that turnout rates for naturalized Latino and Asian American immigrants actually exceeded those for native-born Latinos and Asian Americans. Among Latinos, for example, over 44 percent of immigrants with voting rights took part in the midterms, as opposed to 39 percent of Latinos who were born in the United States.[1]

During the massive immigrant rights demonstrations in the spring of 2006, a common rallying call was, "Today we march, tomorrow we vote!" There is some evidence that these pro-immigrant demonstrations in 2006 helped activate voters for the midterm elections the following November.[2] In the last chapter, we likened the immigrant rights rallies of 2017 in some respects to the 2006 mobilization. Although the surveys at hand do not allow us to draw connections between immigrant engagement in these demonstrations and a

Figure 6.2 *"How Much Have You Thought About the Coming November Election?":* *Latinos' Responses, Summer 2018*

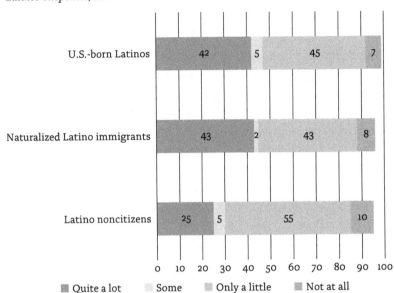

Quite a lot ▪ Some ▪ Only a little ▪ Not at all

Source: Pew Research Center, National Survey of Latinos, fielded between July 26 and September 9, 2018.

Note: N = 696 (U.S.-born Latinos), 302 (naturalized Latinos), and 430 (Latino noncitizens).

heightened tendency to take part in the 2018 midterms, the fact that Latino immigrants were more involved in electoral politics than U.S.-born Latinos suggests such a connection.

To expand on this point, a survey conducted by the Pew Hispanic Center in the summer of 2018 shows the somewhat higher interest in the congressional elections that year among naturalized Latinos than among Latinos born in the United States (figure 6.2). These differences are not large, but there is evidence that in at least some past elections, naturalized Latinos have tended to vote in fewer numbers relative to their U.S.-born counterparts.[3] It appears that the mobilizing forces that prompted deep engagement in the midterm campaigns motivated immigrants at least as much as the native-born.

Even Latino immigrants who were not naturalized U.S. citizens expressed a fair amount of interest in the 2018 midterms. When asked how much they had been thinking about the upcoming election, one out of four noncitizens indicated "quite a lot of thought." Only 10 percent were not paying any attention at all to the campaign at that time. To put these percentages in perspective, in the first wave of the 2016–2017 LINES study (August–September 2016), Latino immigrants were asked how interested they were in the looming presidential contest—very much interested, somewhat interested, or not much interested? Among noncitizen respondents, 28 percent stated that they were not much interested in the campaign, a far higher level of disengagement than in 2018. Although there is no compelling evidence that noncitizens actually vote in federal elections, previous studies have found that immigrants without voting rights often get involved in other, perfectly legal ways, such as encouraging others to support a particular candidate or attending campaign rallies.[4]

Time will tell how involvement in the 2020 election cycle and beyond will compare to 2016 and 2018. As of this writing (mid-2020), there is suggestive evidence that Latino immigrants will continue to take part with as much enthusiasm as U.S.-born Latinos. In an April 2020 survey conducted by the research firm Latino Decisions (N = 1,200), 59 percent of naturalized Latino immigrants indicated that they were "almost certain" to vote in the general election of 2020, and another 17 percent said that they "probably would vote."[5] These percentages are likely to be inflated to an extent; it is one thing to tell a pollster that one is eager to take part, and another to turn out. Nonetheless, this is a strikingly high level of political interest. By comparison, 60 percent of second-generation U.S.-born Latinos stated that they were almost certain to vote, and another 14 percent said that they would probably turn out. It thus appears that, in keeping with patterns of participation from 2018, turnout among naturalized Latino immigrants in the 2020 contest will match or even exceed that for U.S.-born Latinos.

These kinds of trends in immigrant engagement suggest that it would be wise for the Republican Party to revisit its strategic blueprint for expansion following the 2012 presidential election. Recall from the first chapter that this "Growth and Opportunity Project" called for more dedicated outreach to minority constituencies, given the changing demographic makeup of the country. In a 2013 book that purported to "forge a new American solution" to settle the ongoing "immigration wars," former Florida governor Jeb Bush cogently articulated the rationale for such outreach. Bemoaning the fact that there would be no "President Mitt Romney," Bush chastised his fellow Republicans for largely "self-inflicted wounds" at the ballot box.

> Numerous explanations for Romney's defeat came into play, and nearly all of them were demographic. . . . Our nation has experienced rapid and dramatic demographic changes. . . . Over the past decade, minorities have accounted for 85 percent of the nation's population growth. Throughout that time, the Republican Party has clung to its core constituency, seeking to squeeze more votes from an ever-shrinking base. . . . Mitt Romney moved so far to the right on immigration issues that it proved all but impossible for him to appeal to Hispanic voters in the general election. . . . Although Romney eventually called for comprehensive immigration reform, a platform that hardened the party's stance on immigration hung like an anvil around his candidacy.[6]

The election of Donald Trump in 2016 could be interpreted as a sign that Bush's argument and the general thrust of the Growth and Opportunity Project were misplaced. The president himself has certainly made this point time and time again. However, the demographic composition of the electorate in 2018 and the comeback of the Democratic Party that year imply that it would be well to heed the red flags raised among Republican leaders after Romney's loss in 2012. Moreover, it would be wrong to assume that Americans who support President Trump uniformly resonate with his anti-immigrant agenda. In the introductory chapter, we noted that only one-quarter of the voters who backed Trump in the 2016 presidential election wished to see all undocumented immigrants deported from the country, and fewer than half were in favor of building a wall along the southern border of the United States. Responses to a more recent American National Election Study survey conducted in November 2018 are in keeping with these earlier attitudes. In this ANES study, just under 40 percent of respondents stated that they approved of the job President Trump was doing, a percentage that matches other polls on presidential approval conducted at that time.

Among these Trump supporters, *only one-third* consistently backed the president's agenda to build a wall along the southern border, reduce the number of immigrants coming to the United States, and deport all undocumented immigrants. In short, supporters of the president are certainly not all anti-immigrant zealots. However, those Republicans who are most committed to President Trump's anti-immigrant agenda are exceedingly outspoken, even if they are not in the mainstream. If Republican leaders were to move away from their anti-immigrant stance, these nativist elements would probably lash out against the party. Yet over the long run, the Republican Party might have much more to gain than lose by becoming more welcoming toward racial and ethnic minorities and softening its stance on immigration.

We should emphasize that we do not wish to end this book by putting on the hats of Republican Party strategists. As researchers, we instead aim to present a clear empirical sketch of how foreign-born Latinos are responding to the challenges of the post-2016 political environment. Our view is that the immigrants who were tracked in the LINES study are acquitting themselves well. Any loss of faith in governing institutions under the Trump administration does not extend to a rejection of American society on the whole, and immigrants are capable of pushing back against bracing headwinds.

To put a finer point on this pushback, the findings from the preceding three chapters highlight three overarching conclusions about the emotional dimensions of immigrant attitudes toward the federal government and their involvement in political activism. First, feeling angry toward the president and feeling afraid are complementary emotional reactions. One feeling does not undercut the other, but the two feelings appear to be mutually reinforcing in their effects. This result is in keeping with some of the psychological research discussed in the book's second chapter, which holds that negative emotional states often overlap and elicit similar kinds of remediation responses.[7] Immigrants who were both fearful of and angry at Donald Trump were more inclined toward skepticism about governing institutions once Trump was in the White House, relative to those who felt only one such negative emotion or none at all. And anger and fear together prompted immigrants' involvement in forms of civic engagement, such as street protests, while not undercutting their commitment to remaining in the United States or diminishing their trust in Americans.

A second overarching conclusion is that worries about the deportation of friends and family members had more profound effects on political attitudes and activism than anxieties about personal finances. This difference was anticipated in the second chapter. There is a clear connection between the kinds of administrative policies on immigration that government officials pursue and the subsequent risk that a friend or family member may be deported. Consequently, it is understandable that LINES respondents who were concerned about deportations would protest government actions and voice greater skepticism about the trustworthiness of officials. In the case of personal financial woes, however, it would be harder to connect one's worries to specific government policies or the actions of a particular leader such as the president.

A third takeaway is how little these findings vary across the Latino immigrant population. Immigrants who were naturalized citizens, had lived in the country for several decades, resided in a more immigrant-friendly state, or had arrived from a country other than Mexico were about as likely to express concerns about the direction the United States had taken, about the president, and about the well-being of friends and family as immigrants who had no citizenship rights, had not been in the United States for long, lived in a state less supportive of immigrants, or were of Mexican origin. Furthermore, there is strikingly little variation in the effects of the civic stress items on evaluations of governing institutions, attitudes toward the United States in general, and involvement in protest demonstrations. With the Trump administration taking a hard line against immigration in general, aiming to enact policies that would disrupt the lives of even the most deeply rooted immigrants, it may be understandable that even foreign-born Latinos who have more political rights and opportunities would still feel distressed. This suggests that immigrants' responses to the policies of the Trump administration are driven by national, not local, narratives of threat.

If the Republican Party were inclined to follow the advice of Governor Bush, results from the LINES study suggest that Latino immigrants could be responsive. As noted in the previous chapter, the incidence of Democratic Party identification is far higher for this population than Republican identification. In the summer of 2017, nearly four times as many self-identified as Democrats than as Republicans. This should not be taken to mean, however, that Latino immigrants are solidly incorporated into the Democratic Party fold. Indeed, the most prevalent response to the "partisan identification" question was "independent or not sure." As we mentioned at the outset, the fact that Latino immigrants are disenchanted and angry, apprehensive and yet engaged, offers both Democrats and Republicans promise and peril. The promise resides in the fact that Latino immigrants and their children now make up a key part of the American electorate. However, if these new political actors are spurned (as they have been by many Republicans) or taken for granted (as they have sometimes been by Democrats), the peril for both parties is that this part of the electorate could either rebel or sit stubbornly on the sidelines.[8]

The breakdowns in figure 6.3 expand on this theme. Jeb Bush's commentary in *Immigration Wars* notwithstanding, among Latino immigrants the reputations of the two major parties are far from settled. When asked in mid-2017 which party represents the interests of Latinos and immigrants, approximately half of the LINES respondents saw the Democrats as most representative. This is a large margin, of course, but the more noteworthy statistic is that a significant percentage of Latinos in our sample either saw no difference between the parties or were not sure which was more representative. There appears to be a great deal of uncertainty when immigrants consider partisan coalitions and group interests.[9] Meaningful overtures from either party could in principle clarify the parties' positioning. When asked about which party better represents the interests of children, women, and small businesses, the amount of uncertainty and ambivalence reflected in our surveys is greater still. All of this is to demonstrate that even in an era marked by the Trump White House's consistently anti-immigrant rhetoric, Latino immigrants are still not wholeheartedly incorporated into the Democratic Party.

If the hard nativist stance of the Trump presidency leaves a lasting mark on the Republican Party, with party officials and

Figure 6.3 *"Which Party Represents the Interests of . . . ?": Latino Immigrants' Responses, Summer 2017*

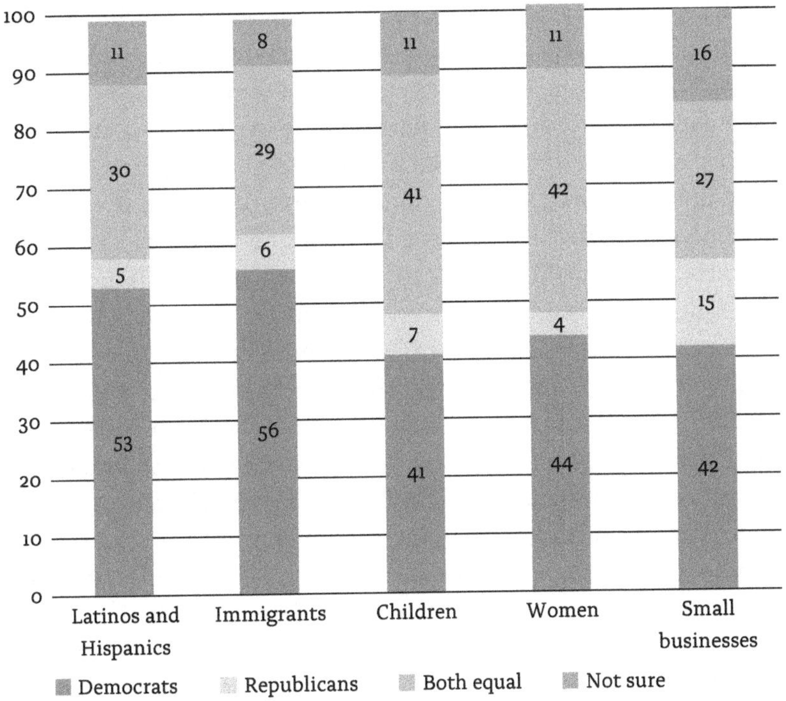

	Democrats	Republicans	Both equal	Not sure
Latinos and Hispanics	53	5	30	11
Immigrants	56	6	29	8
Children	41	7	41	11
Women	44	4	42	11
Small businesses	42	15	27	16

Source: Third wave of 2016–2017 Latino Immigrant National Election Study.

candidates after the Trump years continuing to brand the party as anti-immigrant, immigrants themselves will no doubt move more decisively toward the Democratic Party. The implications of such a move for the representation of immigrant interests, however, would depend on how the Democrats respond to Republican nativism. If the Democratic Party offers a forceful rebuttal and opens up clear pathways for immigrants to stand for higher offices and set the party's policymaking agenda, there could be a genuine expansion of the Democratic base—an expansion that might parallel the kind of ambitious party-building during the New Deal years of the 1930s, when President Roosevelt and national Democratic Party leaders incorporated first- and second-generation immigrants, largely from U.S. cities, into a party whose historic character had been southern, rural, and ethnically homogenous.[10]

On the other hand, if the Republicans were to turn their backs on immigrants and the Democrats were to offer only limited opportunities for meaningful incorporation, immigrants themselves might still side consistently with Democrats during hotly contested political campaigns. But in this scenario of "partisan incorporation by default," their Democratic partisanship might have a decidedly negative cast. That is, immigrants would generally know where they did not belong when it came to party politics in the United States and would still harbor doubts about their true partisan home. Negative partisanship of this sort is increasingly common across the American electorate. One recent analysis notes that U.S. citizens are now far more likely to align themselves *against* one party rather than affiliating *with* the other.[11] Forty years ago, the typical American had a very high opinion of the party with which he or she identified, with scores on 0- to 100-degree "feeling thermometer scales," which measured warmth toward the party, hovering around 70 to 80 degrees; at the same time, their feelings toward the opposition party were lukewarm, in the neighborhood of 40 to 50 degrees. Today there are very different patterns of partisanship. Americans now tend to feel much less warm toward their chosen party—average "thermometer" ratings have fallen to around 60 degrees—even as their "cold" feelings toward the rival party have spiked.

If immigrants were to fall in line with these broad trends, they might remain as politically active as ever. Fear and loathing toward an opponent can motivate much political action. However, would this negative form of Democratic partisanship prompt substantive engagement in the Democratic Party? Would antipathy toward the Republicans in and of itself lead immigrants to take part in important party-building activities for the Democrats, such as attending local party caucuses, answering phones at the party headquarters, canvassing door to door for the party's candidates, and standing for party nominations? Prior research in other political contexts suggests not.[12] People who feel more negative toward an opposition party than positive toward their own may become reliably engaged in political campaigns. But constructive partisan coalition-building at the grass roots is likely to depend on *positive* partisanship—a recognition that one truly belongs in the party, a sense of shared solidarity with other members of the coalition, and a belief that one is reasonably well represented through the party platform.[13]

Since we do not have a crystal ball, all we can do is speculate about the strategic positioning of the two major parties in the near future and consider the implications of these dynamics for immigrant incorporation. Such speculation is warranted, given that the parties are uniquely suited to hear the political voices that rise up from the public and carry them forward into government. The Latino immigrants who took part in the LINES survey reacted quickly to the changing political climate, remained deeply committed to the United States even when concerned about the direction of the country and their own well-being, and continued their engagement in both protests and more conventional political activities. Both parties have a strong incentive, we believe, to pull these engaged immigrants into the party fold. Whether and how the Republicans and Democrats respond to these incentives will determine in no small way the course of immigrant inclusion in American democracy.

Life in the United States in the foreseeable future will be immensely challenging—much more challenging than in the years following the 2016 election. No crystal ball is needed to make this prediction. Mitigation efforts to contain the spread of the Covid-19 virus have sent the U.S. economy into a rapid downward spiral. The pandemic has hit minority groups especially hard, with African Americans and Latinos experiencing higher levels of joblessness and ill health.[14] Foreign-born Latinos are shouldering a particularly heavy burden. In the Latino Decisions survey of April 2020, 40 percent of foreign-born Latino citizens indicated that they or someone in their household had lost a job owing to the virus outbreak; among second-generation U.S.-born Latinos, only 30 percent reported a job loss.[15] Across society at large, economic uncertainties and hardship may lead to xenophobia and increasing prejudice toward ethnic minorities. If respondents from the LINES survey were interviewed again in this climate, they would undoubtedly express even higher levels of anxiety, disappointment, and anger. The resilience and engagement that we highlighted in the preceding chapters make us guardedly optimistic that foreign-born Latinos can weather future storms, holding fast in their attachments to the United States and continuing to raise their voices in politics as the times get tougher. But we recognize that this is highly conjectural—one part social science forecast based on past patterns and trajectories, and one part wishful thinking.

The economic and social dislocations that are sure to come about over the next several years could loosen traditional party coalitions. Might such a loosening mean that the parties become more accessible for immigrants? This would be our hope. We should conclude by saying that this hope is grounded in the practical realities of partisan competition. Many years ago, E. E. Schattschneider, the eminent political scientist we cited in the first chapter, wrote that politics in a democracy is fundamentally about expanding the scope of engagement when times are uncertain and precarious. Political parties, if they are to remain competitive in such moments, should be motivated—almost reflexively—to reach out to new constituencies.[16] The LINES respondents were drawn from such a constituency, one that has shown itself capable of raising its voice under duress while demonstrating loyalty to the country. This constituency, we argue as a final point, is worth competing over rather than shunning.

APPENDIX

SURVEYING IMMIGRANTS: AN OVERVIEW
OF THE LATINO IMMIGRANT NATIONAL
ELECTION STUDIES

Throughout the preceding chapters, we have referred to findings from two original surveys of foreign-born Latinos—the 2012 and 2016–2017 Latino Immigrant National Election Studies. In this appendix, we discuss the sampling strategy for administering the LINES surveys, our approach to addressing potential panel attrition biases in follow-up survey waves, how the panel structure of the data can be leveraged to make sound causal inferences, and the wordings for key items.

Sampling Latino Immigrants

When drawing survey respondents from a population, one should ideally have a comprehensive listing of all eligible study participants— that is, a sampling frame. If registered voters in a particular state are the population of interest, for example, it would be a straightforward exercise, at least in principle, to obtain such a listing from govern- ment records and then gather a sample of respondents at random for interviewing.

For immigrants, however, there is no such off-the-shelf sampling frame. To recruit LINES study participants, we instead sampled from telephone contact lists obtained from marketing research firms, with both cell phone and landline numbers included. In this era of "big data," marketing research firms are able to compile fairly granular profiles of individuals based on their publicly available spending patterns, travel habits, social media postings, social networks, and other kinds of personal information. These databases are far from comprehensive and error-free, and it is not possible to identify with certainty who is or is not foreign-born. But language use is a reasonable proxy indicator for place of birth. We sampled records of Latinos who were said to be bilingual or Spanish-dominant with the expectation that this proxy sampling frame would provide sufficiently wide coverage for the foreign-born Latino population.[1]

The decision to interview immigrants by telephone was born of necessity. Administering surveys in person at an immigrant's place of residence or another location would have been prohibitively expensive. Many major academic surveys nowadays are conducted online. This approach, however, would also not have been advisable for covering the diverse foreign-born Latino population. In a recent overview of surveying methods for ethnic and racial populations, Matt Barreto and his collaborators highlight recent advancements in internet-based interviewing. Online surveys tend to be much less expensive than telephone surveys, which is certainly a virtue, and allowing respondents to react to visual prompts on a screen or tablet rather than just spoken questions from interviewers can be advantageous. However, Barreto and his colleagues note that even with the widespread dissemination of computer technology in recent years, there remains an appreciable digital divide within ethnic communities. Non-English-language-dominant Latinos are difficult to survey via online methods, as are older respondents.[2] For our purposes, then, sampling immigrants through telephone listings was most prudent.

For the 2012 LINES survey, a total of 853 immigrants were randomly recruited for interviewing between October 10 and November 5 of that year, which was right before the general election. Up to fifteen attempts were made to interview each respondent. Interviewers were all highly trained native Spanish speakers with considerable prior experience. Respondents were given the choice of being interviewed in Spanish or English. Nearly all (over 90 percent) chose Spanish. On average, an interview lasted between twenty and twenty-five minutes.

When calculating response rates, it is worth noting that many of the telephone numbers in the fall of 2012 were found to be out of service, dedicated to a fax machine or data line, or chronically busy. In many other instances, an answering machine routinely picked up. If all of these telephone numbers are included when estimating the response rate, the rate is quite low (0.018). The American Association for Public Opinion Research (AAPOR) refers to this calculation as "Response Rate 1." However, when telephone numbers that were found to be out of service or unreachable are omitted from the baseline, the estimated response rate is quite a bit higher at 0.310. And if we gauge the response rate based on the number of respondents who were successfully reached and confirmed to the interviewer that they were indeed Latin America–born and over eighteen years old, nearly all—94.3 percent—agreed to be surveyed. This latter metric is the AAPOR "Cooperation Rate 4" calculation.[3]

Respondents were recruited via similar methods when we fielded the 2016–2017 LINES; this time interviewing took place earlier in the general election campaign (August and September 2016). The 2016–2017 sample was larger than in 2012 (N = 1,800), and nearly all interviews were once again conducted in Spanish. As with the earlier LINES study, many of the initial telephone numbers we dialed were out of service or otherwise unusable. The "Response Rate 1" calculation is therefore correspondingly low (0.034). However, only 12 percent of eligible immigrants, as identified based on the initial screening questions, opted not to complete the survey. As in the 2012 study, interviewers were all native Spanish speakers with extensive professional experience. On average, an interview that fall lasted approximately twenty-five minutes.

In both LINES surveys, the distributions of sociodemographic variables were compared to the relevant American Community Surveys. In most respects, the LINES samples we obtained conformed to the ACS, though significant discrepancies were found for education, age, and gender. In the 2016–2017 study, there was also an overcount of naturalized citizens. Weighting variables were consequently calculated through iterative proportional fitting (that is, "raking").[4] When the LINES data in both studies are weighted, the distributions for educational group, age group, and gender match the ACS. In all of the analyses presented in this book, these weights have been applied.

Addressing Potential Panel Attrition Biases in Follow-up Survey Waves

Shortly after the pre-election survey was concluded in 2012, as many LINES respondents as possible were contacted again for another round of interviewing. This pre-election/post-election survey design was meant to parallel that of the 2012 American National Election Study. In total, 435 immigrants interviewed before the election were successfully interviewed again by the end of the calendar year, for a recontact rate of 51 percent. This rate is less than what is typically obtained in household panel surveys such as the ANES, but it is somewhat better than that in previous election-year telephone panel surveys of the Mexican-born population.[5] When this post-election survey was administered, a fresh sample of 451 respondents was added to the study, using the same sampling methods as before the election. Our interviews with these fresh immigrants allow us to judge the extent of biases in recontacting respondents and to take corrective action.

For the 2016–2017 study, the aim was to draw longer-term inferences about how the Latino immigrant community is responding to a tumultuous turn in American politics. After the 2016 election, 576 immigrants took part in the second survey wave, which was fielded during the presidential transition period (a 32 percent recontact rate). At this time, a fresh sample of 260 Latino immigrants was added to the study—again, to help gauge and ameliorate any potential respondent attrition biases. And finally, in the summer of 2017 (July through early September), a third wave was conducted, with all 1,800 immigrants from the pre-election baseline survey being eligible for interviewing. In this period, 31 percent of these immigrants (N = 554) were surveyed; this included 321 respondents who had taken part in the second wave and 233 who had not. To bring the sample size up at this time and address attrition from one wave to the next, 500 fresh immigrants were surveyed. In total, then, 2,560 immigrants took part in the 2016–2017 LINES: 1,800 from before the election plus 260 during the presidential transition period plus 300 in the summer of 2017.

As would have been expected based on many earlier longitudinal panel surveys, including those few panels that had been conducted within immigrant communities, respondents who were younger and less interested in public affairs were somewhat more likely to drop out of the later post-election waves in 2012 and 2016. These tendencies were not pronounced, but they nonetheless merited attention. To ameliorate any potential attrition biases when modeling the attitude dynamics presented in earlier chapters, and to retain as much information as possible, we followed a "data imputation" strategy: for respondents who dropped out from a subsequent survey wave, plausible survey data values were estimated multiple times based on all available information. The average of these different estimations has been found to be a good representation of what a missing respondent might have reported had he or she been interviewed, assuming that the factors that led the respondent to drop out of the study in the first place are adequately accounted for when calculating these imputations.[6]

This approach to addressing potential panel attrition biases is undeniably preferable to deleting respondents altogether from a particular analysis.[7] All of the results from the LINES surveys reported in this book are based on the full data set. (In other words, missing values were imputed so as to retain all available information.) We should note, however, that even if only complete cases are analyzed (that is, any immigrants who did not report a substantive response to an item are removed), our general inferences about the attitudes and activities of the foreign-born during this time of change and upheaval would be little changed.

Drawing Sound Causal Inferences

Chapters 3, 4, and 5 gauged the effects of pessimism, anger, and anxiety on faith in American governing institutions, attitudes toward the United States in general, and political participation. The panel structure of the 2016–2017 LINES survey allows us to make stronger causal inferences than could be obtained through the analysis of single-shot cross-sectional surveys. If we simply regressed, say, trust in government officials as measured in the summer of 2017 on concerns about the direction that the country was heading, there would probably be a highly significant regression coefficient. The results in figure 3.5 certainly suggest as much. It is possible, however, that some of this apparent effect would be spurious, in that immigrants who are generally distrusting of political authorities might be more pessimistic in the first place about the country being on the "wrong track."

Such potential spuriousness, often labeled endogeneity bias, can be controlled by leveraging the panel structure of the LINES data. The general framework we employ for gauging the impact of a given civic stress measure addresses potential endogeneity biases by taking into account lagged values of the dependent variable as a predictor. In formal terms, the setup for modeling the changes in attitudes discussed in chapters 4 and 5 is: $Attitude_t$ = constant term + $\beta_1(Attitude_{t-1})$ + $\beta_2(Civic\ Stress\ Item_t)$ + effects of the many control variables noted in the figure notes. The logistic regression models to estimate the impacts of pessimism, anger, and anxiety on involvement in immigrant rights protests and marches (chapter 6) follow a similar specification: $Participation_{Summer\ of\ 2017}$ = constant term + $\beta_1(Participation_{Pre-election})$ + $\beta_2(Civic\ Stress\ Item_{Summer\ of\ 2017})$ + effects of controls. If responses to one or another civic stress item depend to any extent on prior values of the dependent variable, estimating the β_1 coefficient factors out this dependency, which in principle leaves us with firmer inferences concerning cause and effect.[8]

The Wordings of Survey Items

The wordings for the LINES items analyzed in chapters 2 through 6 are given here. Whenever possible, we borrowed the bilingual instrumentation from the American National Election Study so as to allow for systematic comparisons of attitude distributions across subpopulations.

COUNTRY ON THE RIGHT OR WRONG TRACK

Do you feel things in this country are generally going in the right direction, or do you feel things have pretty seriously gotten off on the wrong track? / ¿Cree que las cosas en este país están yendo en la dirección correcta o cree que las cosas se han descarrilado bastante hacia el camino equivocado?

1. Right direction / Dirección correcta
2. Wrong track / Camino equivocado

EMOTIONAL REACTIONS TO DONALD TRUMP

Because of the type of person Donald Trump is, or because of something he may have done, have you ever felt anger? / ¿Porque es el tipo de persona que Donald Trump es o por algo que haya hecho, alguna vez le ha hecho sentir enojo?

1. Yes / Sí
2. No / No

Because of the type of person Donald Trump is, or because of something he may have done, have you ever felt fearful? / ¿Porque es el tipo de persona que Donald Trump es o por algo que haya hecho, alguna vez le ha hecho sentir] miedo?

1. Yes / Sí
2. No / No

WORRIES ABOUT DEPORTATION

How worried are you that a close friend or family member may be deported? Extremely worried, very worried, moderately worried, a little worried, or not at all worried? / ¿Qué tanto le preocupa que un amigo cercano o miembro de su familia pudiera ser deportado? ¿Sumamente preocupado, muy preocupado, medianamente preocupado, un poco preocupado o nada?

WORRIES ABOUT FINANCES

So far as you and your family are concerned, how worried are you about your current financial situation? Extremely worried, very worried, moderately worried, a little worried, or not at all worried? / En lo que respecta a usted y su familia, ¿qué tan preocupado está sobre su actual situación financiera? ¿Sumamente preocupado, muy preocupado, medianamente preocupado, un poco preocupado o nada?

TRUST IN GOVERNMENT

How much of the time do you think you can trust the government in Washington to do what is right / ¿Cuánto cree que se puede confiar en que el gobierno de Washington hace lo correcto?

1. Never / Nunca
2. Some of the time / Una vez cada tanto

3. About half the time / Más o menos la mitad de las veces
4. Most of the time / Casi siempre
5. Always / Siempre

BIG INTERESTS IN GOVERNMENT

Would you say the government in Washington is pretty much run by a few big interests looking out for themselves or that it is run for the benefit of all the people? / ¿Diría que el gobierno de Washington está en manos de algunos poderosos grupos de interés que buscan su propio beneficio o es un gobierno para el beneficio de todo el pueblo?

1. Run by a few big interests / En manos de algunos poderosos grupos de interés
2. For the benefit of all the people / Para el beneficio de todo el pueblo

CORRUPTION IN GOVERNMENT

How many of the people running the government in Washington are corrupt? / ¿Cuántos de los funcionarios de gobierno de Washington son corruptos?

1. None / Ninguno
2. A few / Unos pocos
3. About half / Más o menos la mitad
4. Most / La mayoría
5. All / Todos

PLANS TO STAY IN THE UNITED STATES OR TO RETURN TO COUNTRY OF ORIGIN

Do you have plans to return to the country where you were born to live there permanently? / ¿Usted tiene planes para regresar a "su país de origen" para vivir allí permanentemente?

1. Yes / Sí
2. No / No

INTERPERSONAL TRUST

Generally speaking, how often can you trust other people in the United States? / En general, ¿con qué frecuencia puede confiar en otras personas en los Estados Unidos?

1. Never / Nunca
2. Some of the time / Una vez cada tanto
3. About half the time / Más o menos la mitad de las veces
4. Most of the time / Casi siempre
5. Always / Siempre

FEELINGS TOWARD THE U.S. FLAG

When you see the American flag flying, does it make you feel . . . ? / ¿Ver a la bandera estadounidense ondeando le hace sentir . . . ?

1. Extremely good / Sumamente bien
2. Very good / Muy bien
3. Moderately good / Medianamente bien
4. Slightly good / Levemente bien
5. Not good at all / Nada bien

FEELINGS TOWARD THE UNITED STATES

How do you feel about this country? / ¿Qué siente respecto a este país?

1. Hate it / Lo odia
2. Dislike it / Le desagrada
3. Neither like nor dislike it / Le resulta indiferente
4. Like it / Le agrada
5. Love it / Lo ama

PARTICIPATION IN POLITICS: PRE-ELECTION

During the past twelve months, have you . . . / ¿Durante los últimos doce meses, ha . . .

1. Yes/Sí
2. No/No

... Worked with other people to deal with some issue facing your community? / ... Trabajado con otras personas para lidiar con algún problema al que se enfrenta su comunidad?

... Telephoned, written a letter to, or visited a government official to express your views? / ... llamado por teléfono, escrito una carta o visitado a algún funcionario de gobierno para expresar sus opiniones?

... Attended a meeting about an issue facing your community or schools? / ... Asistido a alguna reunión sobre algún problema que enfrenta su comunidad o escuelas?

Over the last three or four months, have you ... / ¿En los últimos tres o cuatro meses, ha ...

1. Yes / Sí
2. No / No

... Gone to political meetings, rallies, speeches, dinners, or things like that? / ... Ido a reuniones políticas, mítines, discursos, cenas, o actividades similares?

PARTICIPATION IN POLITICS: SUMMER 2017

Over the last few months, have you ... / ¿Durante los últimos meses, ha ...

1. Yes / Sí
2. No / No

... Worked with other people to deal with some issue facing your community? / ... Trabajado con otras personas para lidiar con algún problema al que se enfrenta su comunidad?

... Telephoned, written a letter to, or visited a government official to express your views? / ... llamado por teléfono, escrito una carta, o visitado a algún funcionario de gobierno para expresar sus opiniones?

... Attended a meeting about an issue facing your community or schools? / ... Asistido a alguna reunión sobre algún problema que enfrenta su comunidad o escuelas?

... Participated in marches or protests to support immigrants in the United States? / ... Participado en marchas o protestas en el favor de inmigrantes en los Estados Unidos?

INTEREST IN POLITICS

How often do you pay attention to what's going on in government and politics? Always, most of the time, about half the time, some of the time, or never? / ¿Con qué frecuencia presta atención a asuntos de gobierno y política? Siempre, casi siempre, más o menos la mitad de las veces, a veces o nunca?

POLITICS TOO COMPLICATED

"Sometimes, politics and government seem so complicated that a person like me can't really understand what's going on." / "A veces, las cuestiones políticas y de gobierno parecen tan complicadas que una persona como yo no puede comprender qué está pasando en realidad."

1. Agree strongly / Totalmente de acuerdo
2. Agree somewhat / Algo de acuerdo
3. Neither agree nor disagree / Ni de acuerdo ni en desacuerdo
4. Disagree somewhat / Algo en desacuerdo
5. Disagree strongly / Totalmente en desacuerdo

GOOD UNDERSTANDING OF POLITICS

"I feel that I have a pretty good understanding of the important political issues facing our country." / "Creo que entiendo bastante bien los problemas políticos importantes que enfrenta nuestro país."

1. Agree strongly / Totalmente de acuerdo
2. Agree somewhat / Algo de acuerdo
3. Neither agree nor disagree / Ni de acuerdo ni en desacuerdo
4. Disagree somewhat / Algo en desacuerdo
5. Disagree strongly / Totalmente en desacuerdo

PARTY IDENTIFICATION

Generally speaking, do you usually think of yourself as a Democrat, a Republican, an independent, or what? / En términos generales, ¿usted se considera demócrata, republican, independiente u otra cosa?

(*If partisan*) Would you call yourself a strong [Democrat / Republican] or a not very strong [Democrat / Republican]? / ¿Se considera fuertemente [demócrata / republicano] o no muy fuertemente [demócrata / republicano]?

(*If not partisan*) Do you think of yourself as closer to the Republican Party or to the Democratic Party? / ¿Usted se considera más cercano al Partido Republicano o al Partido Demócrata?

LATINO/HISPANIC IDENTIFICATION

Which of the following words would you use to describe yourself? Hispanic? Latino? / ¿Cuál de las siguientes palabras usaría usted para describirse a sí mismo? Hispano(a)? Latino(a)?

IMMIGRATION POLICY PREFERENCE

Which comes closest to your view about what government policy should be toward unauthorized immigrants now living in the United States? / ¿Qué opción se acerca más a lo que usted opina sobre cuál debería ser la política del gobierno respecto a los inmigrantes que viven ahora en Estados Unidos sin autorización?

1. Make all unauthorized immigrants felons and send them back to their home country. / Considerar a todos los inmigrantes sin autorización delincuentes y mandarlos de vuelta a su país de origen.
2. Have a guest worker program that allows unauthorized immigrants to remain in the United States in order to work, but only for a limited amount of time. / Tener un programa de trabajadores extranjeros que permita que los inmigrantes sin autorización se queden en Estados Unidos a trabajar, pero solo por un tiempo limitado.
3. Allow unauthorized immigrants to remain in the United States and eventually qualify for U.S. citizenship, but only if they meet

certain requirements like paying back taxes and fines, learning English, and passing background checks. / Ermitir que los inmigrantes sin autorización permanezcan en Estados Unidos y que a la larga califiquen para la ciudadanía estadounidense, pero solo si reúnen ciertos requisitos como pagar impuestos y multas, aprender inglés y pasar los controles de antecedentes.

4. Allow unauthorized immigrants to remain in the United States and eventually qualify for U.S. citizenship, without penalties. / Permitir que los inmigrantes sin autorización permanezcan en Estados Unidos y que a la larga califiquen para ser ciudadanos estadounidenses, sin sanciones.

VOTED BEFORE EMIGRATING

Before coming to the United States, did you sometimes vote in the country where you were born? / ¿Antes de venir a los EE.UU., votó alguna vez en las elecciones de su país de origen?

1. Yes / Sí
2. No / No

PARTY REPRESENTATIVENESS

Talking now about the political parties, which party do you think does a better job looking out for the interests of . . . / Hablando de los partidos políticos, qué partido cree que hace un mejor trabajo a la hora de proteger los intereses de . . .

1. Democratic Party / Partido demócrata
2. Republican Party / Partido republicano
3. Both equal / Ambos son iguales

Women / Mujeres
Latinos and Hispanics / Latinos e hispanos
Children / Niños
Small businesses / Pequeños negocios
Immigrants / Inmigrantes

CIVIC STATUS

Are you a naturalized citizen in the United States? / ¿Es usted ciudadano naturalizado en Estados Unidos?

1. Yes / Sí
2. No / No

(*If not*) Do you have a "mica," that is, a green card? / ¿Tiene Ud. una mica ("green card")?

1. Yes / Sí
2. No / No

TIME IN THE UNITED STATES

When did you come to live in the United States for the first time? (*Mark the year in four digits, 1918–2017*)
¿Cuándo vino a vivir a EE. UU. (continental) por primera vez? (*Registre el año en cuatro dígitos, 1918–2017*)

AGE

In what year were you born? / ¿En qué año nació usted?

GENDER

(*Not asked but noted*)

EDUCATION LEVEL

What is the highest level of school you have completed or the highest degree you have received? / ¿Cuál es el último nivel de educación que completó o el título más alto que ha obtenido?

1. Less than first grade / Menos que el primer grado
2. First, second, third, or fourth grade / Primer, segundo, tercer o cuarto grado

3. Fifth or sixth grade / Quinto o sexto grado
4. Seventh or eighth grade / Séptimo o octavo grado
5. Ninth grade / Noveno grado
6. Tenth grade / Décimo grado
7. Eleventh grade / Onceavo grado
8. Twelfth grade, no diploma / Duodécimo grado, sin diploma
9. High school graduate, high school diploma or equivalent (for example, GED) / Graduado de escuela secundaria, diploma de preparatoria o equivalente (por ejemplo, GED)
10. Some college but no degree / Universidad incomplete
11. Associate degree in college, occupational or vocational program / Título de dos años en una universidad, programa ocupacional o vocacional
12. Associate degree in college, academic program / Título de dos años en una universidad, programa académico
13. Bachelor's degree (for example, BA, AB, BS) / Título de licenciado (por ejemplo, BA, AB, BS)
14. Master's degree (for example, MA, MS, MEng, MEd, MSW, MBA) / Maestría (por ejemplo, MA, MS, MEng, MEd, MSW, MBA)
15. Professional school degree (for example, MD, DDS, DVM, LLB, JD) / Título de posgrado (por ejemplo, MD, DDS, DVM, LLB, JD)
16. Doctorate degree (for example, PhD, EdD) / Doctorado (por ejemplo, PhD, EdD)

FAMILY INCOME

Talking more about your situation, what was your total combined household income in 2016 [or 2017] before taxes? This question is completely confidential and just used to help classify the responses, but it is very important to our study. Just stop me when I read the correct category. / Hablando más de su situación, cuál fue su ingreso total de su hogar combinado en 2016 [o 2017] antes de impuestos? Esta pregunta es totalmente confidencial y solo utilizada para ayudar a clasificar las respuestas, pero es muy importante para nuestra investigación. Deténgame cuando le lea la categoría correcta.

1. Less than $20,000 / Menos de $20,000
2. $20,000 to less than $40,000 / Desde $20,000 y menos de $40,000

3. $40,000 to less than $60,000 / Desde $40,000 y menos de $60,000

4. $60,000 to less than $80,000 / Desde $60,000 y menos de $80,000

5. $80,000 to less than $100,000 / Desde $80,000 y menos de $100,000

6. $100,000 to less than $150,000 / Desde $100,000 y menos de $150,000

7. More than $150,000 / Mas de $150,000

LANGUAGE USE AT HOME

What language do you primarily speak at home with your family? / ¿Qué idioma habla principalmente en su casa con su familia?

1. Only English / Solo inglés
2. Mostly English /Principalmente inglés
3. Both languages equally / Ambos idiomas por igual
4. Mostly Spanish / Principalmente español
5. Only Spanish / Solo español

ATTENDANCE AT RELIGIOUS SERVICES

How often do you go to religious services? / ¿Con qué frecuencia asiste a servicios religiosos?

1. Every week or more / Todas las semanas o más
2. Almost every week / Casi todas las semanas
3. Once or twice a month / Una o dos veces al mes
4. A few times a year / Unas pocas veces al año
5. Never / Nunca

MARITAL STATUS

Are you now married, widowed, divorced, separated, or never married? (*If respondent answers "married" without mentioning that spouse is absent, code 1.*) / ¿Está usted casado, viudo, divorciado, separado, o nunca se ha casado? (*Si el encuestado responde "casado" sin decir que su cónyuge está ausente, asigne el código 1.*)

1. Married: spouse present / Casado: cónyuge presente
2. Married: spouse absent (*volunteered*) / Casado: cónyuge ausente (*no lea*)
3. Widowed / Viudo
4. Divorced / Divorciado
5. Separated / Separado
6. Never married / Nunca se ha casado

HOMEOWNERSHIP

Do you or your family own your home, pay rent, or do something else? / ¿Usted o su familia tiene vivienda propia, alquila o está en otra situación?

1. Own home / Tiene vivienda propia
2. Pay rent / Alquila
3. Other (*specify*) / Otra (*especifique*)

COUNTRY OF ORIGIN

In which country were you born? / ¿En qué país nació usted?

1. Argentina
2. Bolivia
3. Chile
4. Colombia
5. Costa Rica
6. Cuba
7. Dominican Republic / República Dominicana
8. Ecuador
9. El Salvador
10. Guatemala
11. Honduras
12. Mexico / México

13. Nicaragua
14. Panama / Panamá
15. Paraguay
16. Peru / Perú
17. Puerto Rico
18. Spain / España
19. Uruguay
20. Venezuela

NOTES

Chapter 1: Introduction: An Emerging Bipartisan Consensus on Immigration Is Disrupted

1. References to immigrants or immigration came up 364 times in Trump's speeches; the two next most salient topics were African Americans (230 mentions) and workers (217 mentions). See Lamont, Park, and Ayala-Hurtado 2017.

2. Jeb Bush, an early front-runner for the 2016 Republican presidential nomination, stands out especially in this regard, in that he had recently published a book calling for comprehensive immigration policy reform to allow undocumented immigrants to remain in the country.

3. See Barber and McCarty 2015; Carter et al. 2008; Wroe 2008; and D'Antonio, Tuch, and Baker 2013.

4. Lauter 2012; Shear and Gabriel 2012.

5. See, for example, Carey et al. 2019; Miller and Quealy 2017; Lawless and Fox 2018.

6. Schildkraut 2007.

7. Ngai 2004, 23.

8. Radford 2019.

9. Schildkraut 2007; Theiss-Morse 2009.

10. On long-term trends in public opinion regarding immigration, see Hainmueller and Hopkins 2014; Muste 2013.

11. In "Confronting Asymmetric Polarization," Jacob Hacker and Paul Pierson (2015) examine other issue areas where partisan positioning tends to be asymmetric.

12. These preferences were out of sync with the more moderate and welcoming signals that Republican president George W. Bush wished to send from the White House at that time.

13. The time series studies are available by year at the ANES website: https://election studies.org/.

14. Results of these Gallup polls are available at https://news.gallup.com/poll/1660 /immigration.aspx. Interestingly, Gallup tracking polls show that support for immigration has risen slightly during the Trump administration.

15. Downs 1957, 28.

16. Republican National Committee 2015, 4.
17. Ibid., 10.
18. Cohen et al. 2008.
19. Bush and Bolick 2013.
20. *Washington Post* 2015.
21. Sides, Tesler, and Vavreck 2018a, 2.
22. Lamont, Park, and Ayala-Hurtado 2017.
23. Sides, Tesler, and Vavreck 2018b.
24. Pierce, Bolter, and Selee 2018.
25. For information on DACA, see the DHS website: https://www.dhs.gov /deferred-action-childhood-arrivals-daca (last updated September 23, 2019).
26. Tenpas, McCann, and Charnock 2018.
27. Kreis 2017.
28. See, for example, Schlozman, Verba, and Brady 2012.
29. Schattschneider 1969, 43.
30. See, for example, Almond and Verba 1963.
31. According to the most recent estimates, just over half (52 percent) of immigrants in the United States are Latin American in origin. Nearly one-third (31 percent) emigrated from one of the Asian countries. Five percent are African-origin, and 11 percent came from Europe. See Migration Policy Institute, "Regions of Birth for Immigrants in the United States, 1960–Present," https://www.migrationpolicy .org/programs/data-hub/us-immigration-trends#source.

Chapter 2: Living Civic Life on the Edge: The Effects of Disappointment and Vulnerability on Immigrant Political Incorporation

1. Lench et al. 2019.
2. Dooling 2016.
3. Koumpilova and Mahamud 2016.
4. Gumbel 2016.
5. See the appendix for more technical details concerning the LINES panel survey and our method for addressing potential nonresponse biases.
6. See PollingReport.com for extensive compilations of polling results for this item.
7. Overall, the average level of worrying on the four-point scale rose from 2.64 (2013) to 2.81 (2018), a shift that is statistically significant ($p = .02$); this amount of change equates to nearly one-fifth of a pooled standard deviation. These Pew surveys are publicly archived at https://www.pewresearch.org/hispanic /data-and-resources/. See also Lopez et al. 2013; Lopez, Gonzalez-Barrera, and Krogstad 2018. N = 361 Latino immigrants in 2013 and 734 in 2018.
8. In the post-election transition period, the correlation between these two items is 0.23; in the third wave of the LINES survey, this correlation is slightly lower at 0.19.

9. Indeed, only *1 percent* of the LINES sample in the summer of 2017 stated that they thought the country was on the right track, were not worried about deportations or family finances, and had no negative emotional reactions to the president.

10. Enchautegui and Giannarelli 2015; Pastor and Scoggins 2012.

11. As noted in the technical appendix, the LINES sample was weighted so that the proportions of naturalized citizens, legal permanent residents, and noncitizens without a green card matched those in U.S. census estimates for foreign-born Latinos over eighteen: 36 percent citizen; 33 percent legal permanent resident; and 31 percent neither citizen nor legal permanent resident.

12. These are some of the conclusions drawn from an extensive recent analysis of immigrant integration; see National Academies of Sciences, Engineering, and Medicine 2015.

13. Ibid., 3.

14. Reich 2018.

15. E-Verify is an online website maintained by the Department of Homeland Security where employers can check on the employment eligibility of potential hires.

16. Gulasekaram and Ramakrishnan 2015.

17. Monogan 2013.

18. See, for example, Lee 2015.

19. Donald Trump is hardly the first commentator to look disapprovingly at the Mexican-born population. Indeed, anti-Mexican sentiment runs deep in American history and at times has led to deadly consequences. See Carrigan and Webb 2013; Martinez 2018.

20. These percentages are predictions based on an ordered logistic regression model, where evaluations of the direction of the United States are regressed on the number of years a respondent had lived in the country.

21. We again use ordered logistic regression to calculate predicted percentages of political disappointment.

22. Libell and Porter 2018.

23. Asad L. Asad offers a similar observation in "Why Latino Citizens Are Worrying More About Deportation" (2020). It is possible that the impact of anger, fear, and disappointment on political attitudes and behavior varies depending on how long an immigrant has lived in the United States, whether or not he or she is a naturalized citizen, whether or not the state of residence is welcoming toward immigrants, and whether or not he or she is Mexican-origin. Such variations are considered in the next three chapters. This line of inquiry parallels that in Davin Phoenix's recent work *The Anger Gap: How Race Shapes Emotion in Politics* (2019). Phoenix argues that angry feelings about politics prompt less activism among African Americans relative to whites owing to the historically marginalized status of African Americans in U.S. society.

24. Easton 1965, 124.

25. Almond and Verba 1963, 63.

26. Sullivan and Transue 1999.

27. Parker 2010.

28. In various municipalities across the United States, noncitizens are eligible to vote in local elections (see Hayduk 2006). The design of the Latino Immigrant National Election Studies would not allow us to track those few survey respondents who may have taken part in such local municipal elections.

29. The scholarly literature in this field is voluminous. See, for example, Neuman et al. 2007; Tolchin 1999; Aytac and Stokes 2019; and Valentino et al. 2011. For an engaging discussion of how some people may become animated and more accepting of risk when they feel deeply aggrieved about their personal situation, see Safire 1992.

30. See, for example, Albertson and Gadarian 2015; Huddy, Feldman, and Cassese 2007; Valentino et al. 2008; and Marcus and MacKuen 1993. In one recent study, Lonna Rae Atkeson and Cherie Maestas (2012) show that when individuals simply observe others with whom they identify suffering the effects of a natural catastrophe, such as Hurricane Katrina, they grow anxious themselves and follow politics more closely.

31. Kurtzleben 2016

32. Aytac and Stokes 2019, 34.

33. See, for example, Watson and Tellegen 1985.

34. Kinder and Kiewiet 1981, 158.

35. Feldman 1982; Lau and Sears 1981.

36. Gomez and Wilson 2006.

Chapter 3: The Effect of Civic Stress on Faith in American Government: Less Tint in the Rose-Colored Glasses?

1. Warren 2017, 48.

2. Tyler 1990.

3. Shames 2017.

4. Almond and Verba 1963.

5. Norris 1999.

6. James Madison's *Federalist 10* appeared in Publius, *The Federalist Papers*, a series of essays written by the framers and published November 22, 1787.

7. On this point, see Samuel P. Huntington, *American Politics: The Promise of Disharmony* (Cambridge, MA: Harvard University Press, 1981).

8. Citrin and Stoker 2018.

9. Hetherington 2015.

10. Marcus, MacKuen, and Neuman 2000.

11. Michelson 2003, 924; see also Abrajano and Alvarez 2010.

12. See, for example, Maxwell 2010; Röder and Mühlau 2011.

13. Festinger 1957. Cognitive dissonance theory posits that individuals experience psychological distress when challenged to hold two or more contradictory beliefs or values. To relieve this stress, one of the beliefs or values is changed so there is no longer any contradiction.

14. Citrin and Stoker 2018.

15. When Americans consider what is or is not corrupt in politics, they are generally mindful of not only overtly illegal activities in government but also actions that violate widely recognized ethical and social norms. See Redlawsk and McCann 2005.

16. Before calculating these percentages and estimating the regression findings that are presented in later figures, missing responses were imputed (see the technical appendix for further methodological details). Imputing missing values allows us to retain all immigrants in the study, which can counteract potential attrition biases and maximizes statistical "efficiency" when estimating the effects of anger, pessimism, and worries.

17. Zaller and Feldman 1992.

18. Dummy variables measure qualitative "either/or" distinctions among respondents. In the case of emotional reactions to Donald Trump, four dummies cover the range of emotions: anger toward Trump; fear because of Trump; both anger and fear; and neither anger nor fear. This last category—no negative reactions—serves as the baseline for gauging the relative impact of each kind of emotional response.

19. The background traits taken into account when gauging the effects of civic stress include civic status (whether the immigrant was a U.S. citizen, a legal permanent resident with a green card, or a noncitizen without a green card); the number of years that the immigrant had lived in the United States; age; gender; level of formal education; family income; language use at home; attendance at religious services; whether or not the immigrant owned a home; the degree to which the respondent's state of residence was welcoming or unwelcoming toward immigrants (based on the scale in figure 2.5); and whether or not the respondent was born in Mexico. All of these traits have been linked in past research to the attitudes and political aspirations of immigrants. It is therefore fitting to take them into account when examining impressions of the federal government. "Lagged values" of the dependent variable were also included as a predictor in each regression model. For example, when calculating the effect of, say, pessimism about the direction of the country on levels of trust in government officials during the presidential transition period, the respondent's degree of trust as measured in the preceding (pre-election) survey wave was factored in. As discussed in the appendix, taking into account lagged values of the dependent variable in this way bolsters our claims about cause and effect.

20. Interaction effects are gauged by adding multiplicative terms to the regression model as predictors (for example, worries about deportation multiplied by length of time in the United States). When probing for such interactions, we allowed the stability of attitude judgments from one wave to the next to vary based on time in the United States (in the first set of models), naturalization status (in the second set), state-level policy disposition toward immigrants (third set), and whether or not the respondent had emigrated from Mexico (fourth set).

Chapter 4: Immigrant Attachments to American Society: Holding Fast?

1. *Federal Register* 26:203 (October 20, 1961), §243.4, 9859.
2. CNN News 1993.
3. Safire 1994, 78.
4. Madison 2012.
5. Beckwith 2016.
6. Massey et al. 1993.
7. Alvarado 2018.
8. C-SPAN Archives 2013.
9. Valdez, Valentine, and Padilla 2013; see also Wampler, Chávez, and Pedraza 2009.
10. The results of an analysis by Magnus Lofstrom, Sarah Bohn, and Steven Raphael (2011) of the effects of a separate 2007 Arizona law that required all state employers to confirm the eligibility of workers through the federal E-Verify database speak to this point. These authors find two main consequences. First, there was a measurable decline in the undocumented population as many immigrants relocated to other U.S. states rather than return to their country of origin. And second, a large number of undocumented immigrants were driven further into Arizona's informal economy, an outcome that was certainly at odds with what lawmakers intended.
11. Putnam 2000; Almond and Verba 1963.
12. The R^2 of 0.98 in this regression model indicates that yearly upticks in the foreign-born population lay almost perfectly along the fitted line.
13. We recognize that a simple regression analysis such as this cannot capture what might be substantial shifts in the composition of the foreign-born population. Undocumented migration to the United States has declined in recent years, for example, while the number of asylum-seekers has increased. Furthermore, in the years ahead, it is possible that the foreign-born population in the United States will actually contract rather than continue to expand, especially if the harsh anti-immigrant policies of the White House remain in place. One recent study hints at such a contraction, owing to a trend in reverse migration among Mexicans; see Warren 2020.
14. Fraga et al. 2013.
15. Wampler, Chávez, and Pedraza 2009.
16. Since most of the respondents in this post-election survey were part of the pre-election LINES wave, it is worth noting that responses to the "return or remain" item in that initial wave do not correlate significantly with panel attrition. That is, before the election immigrants who mentioned having plans to repatriate were no more difficult to locate and interview again in the second wave than those who intended to stay in the country permanently. Moreover, plans to return or remain as measured in the transition period do not correlate with panel attrition in the third wave of the LINES panel. As with earlier analyses, missing data values in the 2016–2017 LINES panel were imputed so that all respondents are retained. Our inferences about repatriation plans, however, would be largely the same if cases with missing data were discarded.

17. Regressing these preference as gauged in the presidential transition wave of the panel on this same item from the first wave before the election yields a continuity estimate of 0.46—far from a perfect 1.0, but indicative of more stability than the attitudes toward the federal government that were modeled in the last chapter (figure 3.4). The continuity in long-term residential plans between the second and third panel waves was even higher, with a regression estimate of 0.52.

18. When calculating the impact of one or another of the stress items, we also control for several personal and demographic factors (civic status, number of years living in the United States, age, gender, education, family income, language use at home, attendance at religious services, marital status, home-ownership, state-level policy disposition toward immigrants, and whether or not the respondent emigrated from Mexico).

19. For Pew Research Center's 2018 National Survey of Latinos, see https://www.pewhispanic.org/dataset/2018-national-survey-of-latinos/.

20. See, for example, Wilkes and Wu 2018.

Chapter 5: Raising Voices in Response to Civic Stress: How Many Decibels?

1. To protect privacy, we have used a pseudonym. These reflections on the 2006 immigrant rights mobilization were discussed in an interview with McCann on September 9, 2014.

2. For an analysis of labor market demand and Mexican settlement in "new" immigrant destinations in the Midwest and South in the 1990s and early 2000s, see Zúñiga and Hernández-León 2005.

3. See Eig and Krouse 1998.

4. Coyne 2006.

5. Bada et al. 2006; Wallace, Jones-Correa, and Zepeda-Millán 2016; Bada et al. 2010.

6. Bloemraad, Voss, and Lee 2011.

7. Zepeda-Millán 2017, 60.

8. Verba, Schlozman, and Brady 1995, 269.

9. See Sears, Danbold, and Zavala 2016; McCann and Nishikawa Chávez 2016. Hajnal and Lee (2011) and Wong (2006) chart levels of partisanship among immigrants but fault the party system for not being more inclusive.

10. Rosenblum 2008, 338–39.

11. See, for example, Min 2014; Jones-Correa and Leal 1996.

12. Uhlaner, Cain, and Kiewiet 1989; see also Leal 2002.

13. Jones-Correa 1998.

14. Putnam 2000.

15. See Somerville, Durana, and Terrazas 2008; Bada 2014.

16. See Wong 2006; Jones-Correa 1998.

17. See Leal, Patterson, and Tafoya 2016.

18. For a fuller description of the counting algorithm, see Count Love, https://countlove.org/faq.html.

19. As in chapters 3 and 4, potential variations in effects were assessed by adding interaction terms to the regression models. In no case do we find that a particular civic stress item interacted significantly with citizenship status, years spent in the United States, state of residence, or Mexican origin.

20. See, for example, Crozier, Huntington, and Watanuki 1975.

Chapter 6: Conclusion: Will Immigrant Voices Be Heard?

1. Krogstad, Noe-Bustamante, and Flores 2019. On differences in participation rates across immigrant generations, see Potochnick and Stegmaier 2020. In the 2020 election cycle, a record high number of eligible voters will be foreign-born. If immigrants continue to turn out in greater numbers, their impact on the outcome could be quite consequential. See Budiman, Noe-Bustamante, and Lopez 2020.

2. See, for example, Pantoja, Menjívar, and Magaña 2008.

3. Barreto 2005.

4. See Leal 2002; Jones-Correa and McCann 2013. On the unproven allegations that undocumented immigrants are voting in federal elections, see Cohn 2017; Ansolabehere, Luks, and Schaffner 2015.

5. See, Latino Decisions, SOMOS Covid-19 Crisis National Latino Survey, April 2020, https://latinodecisions.com/polls-and-research/somos-covid-19 -crisis-national-latino-survey-april-2020/.

6. Bush and Bolick 2013, 199–200.

7. Aytac and Stokes 2019; Watson and Tellegen 1985.

8. Barrón-López and Schneider 2020.

9. These findings accord with the discussions in Hajnal and Lee (2011) and Morin, Mejia, and Sanchez (2020).

10. On party-building in the New Deal era, see Andersen 1979. Research conducted in California following the Republican Party–backed Proposition 187 ballot initiative in 1994 suggests that just such a partisan realignment occurred within that state. Recall from chapter 4 that this proposition would have denied all public services to undocumented immigrants and forced state employees to turn over undocumented immigrants to the Immigration and Naturalization Service for immediate deportation. In the aftermath of the Proposition 187 ballot initiative and related anti-immigrant measures that Republicans pursued at that time, first- and second-generation immigrants moved solidly into the Democratic camp, thereby helping to turn the state reliably "blue" in elections. See, for example, Pantoja, Ramirez, and Segura 2001; Dyck, Johnson, and Wasson 2012; Barreto 2005.

11. Abramowitz and Webster 2018.

12. See, for example, Caruana, McGregor, and Stephenson 2015.

13. Rosenblum 2008.

14. Cava 2020; Jordan and Oppel 2020.

15. Latino Decisions, SOMOS Covid-19 Crisis National Latino Survey, April 2020.

16. Schattschneider 1975.

Appendix: Surveying Immigrants: An Overview of the Latino Immigrant National Election Studies

1. To illustrate, the marketing research firm Geoscape—our source for many of the telephone numbers for both election cycles—created a "Hispanicity" index to categorize Latinos based on their level of acculturation and language use. From this list, we were able to identify prospective respondents who were likely to have been born outside of the United States, concentrating in particular on targeting study participants in neighborhoods of higher Latino density. On the challenges of surveying immigrants without preexisting sampling frames, see Reichel and Morales (2017) and Berry, Chouhoud, and Junn (2018).

2. Barreto et al. 2018, 178.

3. See American Association for Public Opinion Research, "Response Rates— An Overview," https://www.aapor.org/Education-Resources/For-Researchers /Poll-Survey-FAQ/Response-Rates-An-Overview.aspx.

4. This "raking" approach is described in Deville, Sarnda, and Sautory 1993.

5. McCann, Leal, and Cornelius 2009.

6. Rubin 1987. Regarding the use of missing data imputation strategies to ameliorate potential attrition biases in panel surveys, as we do here, see Deng et al. 2013. In total, one hundred completed data sets were imputed. This is a far greater number of imputed data sets than is typical, but it is warranted in this case. On this point, see Allison 2012.

7. The Amelia software package introduced in King et al. (2001) was used for imputing missing data values.

8. On this point, see Finkel 1995; Bartels 2006.

REFERENCES

Abrajano, Marisa, and R. Michael Alvarez. 2010. "Assessing the Causes and Effects of Political Trust Among U.S. Latinos." *American Politics Research* 38(1, January): 110–41.

Abramowitz, Alan I., John McGlennon, Ronald B. Rapoport, and Walter J. Stone. 2001. *Activists in the United States Presidential Nomination Process, 1980–1996*. ICPSR06143-v2. Ann Arbor, Mich.: Inter-university Consortium for Political and Social Research (distributor). DOI: 10.3886/ICPSR06143.v2.

Abramowitz, Alan, and Steven W. Webster. 2018. "Negative Partisanship: Why Americans Dislike Parties but Behave Like Rabid Partisans." *Political Psychology* 39(S1, February): 119–35.

Albertson, Bethany, and Shana Kushner Gadarian. 2015. *Anxious Politics: Democratic Citizenship in a Threatening World*. New York: Cambridge University Press.

Allison, Paul. 2012. "Why You Probably Need More Imputations than You Think." Statistical Horizons, November 9. https://statisticalhorizons.com/more-imputations.

Almond, Gabriel, and Sidney Verba. 1963. *The Civic Culture: Political Attitudes and Democracy in Five Nations*. Princeton, N.J.: Princeton University Press.

Alvarado, Monsy. 2018. "As Trump Crackdown Continues, More Undocumented Immigrants Are Choosing to Self-Deport." *USA Today, North Jersey*, April 27. https://www.northjersey.com/story/news/2018/04/27/trump-crackdown -continues-more-undocumented-immigrants-choosing-self-deport/547939002/.

Andersen, Kristi. 1979. *The Creation of a Democratic Majority, 1928–1936*. Chicago: University of Chicago Press.

Ansolabehere, Stephen. 2012. *Cooperative Congressional Election Study, 2006*. ICPSR 30141-v1. Ann Arbor, Mich.: Inter-university Consortium for Political and Social Research (distributor), March 26. DOI: 10.3886/ICPSR30141.v1.

Ansolabehere, Stephen, Samantha Luks, and Brian F. Schaffner. 2015. "The Perils of Cherry Picking Low Frequency Events in Large Sample Surveys." *Electoral Studies* 40: 409–10.

Asad, Asad L. 2020. "Why Latino Citizens Are Worrying More About Deportation." *The Conversation*, April 6. https://theconversation.com/why-latino-citizens -are-worrying-more-about-deportation-133216.

Atkeson, Lonna Rae, and Cherie Maestas. 2012. *Catastrophic Politics: How Extraordinary Events Redefine Perceptions of Government*. New York: Cambridge University Press.

Aytac, S. Erdem, and Susan C. Stokes. 2019. *Why Bother? Rethinking Participation in Elections and Protests*. New York: Cambridge University Press.

Bada, Xóchitl. 2014. *Mexican Hometown Associations in Chicagoacán*. New Brunswick, N.J.: Rutgers University Press.

Bada, Xóchitl, Jonathan Fox, Andrew Selee, and Robert Donnelly. 2010. *Context Matters: Latino Immigrant Civic Engagement in Nine U.S. Cities*. Washington, D.C.: Woodrow Wilson International Center for Scholars. https://www.wilsoncenter.org/sites/default/files/media/documents/publication/Context%20Matters.pdf.

Bada, Xóchitl, Jonathan Fox, Elvia Zazueta, and Ingrid García. 2006. "2006 Immigration Marches Database." Washington, D.C.: Mexico Institute, Woodrow Wilson International Center for Scholars. https://www.wilsoncenter.org/publication/2006-immigration-marches-database.

Barber, Michael, and Nolan McCarty. 2015. "Causes and Consequences of Polarization." In *Political Negotiation: A Handbook*, edited by Jane Mansbridge and Cathie Jo Martin. Washington, D.C.: Brookings Institution Press.

Barreto, Matt. 2005. "Latino Immigrants at the Polls: Foreign-Born Voter Turnout in the 2002 Election." *Political Research Quarterly* 58(1, March): 79–86.

Barreto, Matt A., Lorrie Frasure-Yokley, Edward D. Vargas, and Janelle Wong. 2018. "Best Practices in Collecting Online Data with Asian, Black, Latino, and White Respondents: Evidence from the 2016 Collaborative Multiracial Post-Election Survey." *Politics, Groups, and Identities* 6(1): 171–80.

Barrón-López, Laura, and Elena Schneider. 2020. "Biden's Latino Outreach Is Under Fire: 'I Can't Tell What Their Strategy Is.'" *Politico*, May 14. https://www.politico.com/news/2020/05/14/joe-biden-latino-outreach-255282.

Bartels, Larry M. 2006. "Three Virtues of Panel Data for the Analysis of Campaign Effects." In *Capturing Campaign Effects*, edited by Henry E. Brady and Richard Johnston. Ann Arbor: University of Michigan Press.

Beckwith, Ryan Teague. 2016. "Read the Full Transcript of the Tenth Republican Debate in Texas." *Time Magazine*, February 26.

Berry, Justin, Youssef Chouhoud, and Jane Junn. 2018. "Reaching Beyond Low-Hanging Fruit: Surveying Low-Incidence Populations." In *Oxford Handbook of Polling and Survey Methods*, edited by Lonna Rae Atkeson and R. Michael Alvarez. New York: Oxford University Press.

Bloemraad, Irene, Kim Voss, and Taeku Lee. 2011. "The Protests of 2006: What Were They, How Do We Understand Them, Where Do We Go?" In *Rallying for Immigrant Rights: The Fight for Inclusion in 21st Century America*, edited by Kim Voss and Irene Bloemraad. Berkeley: University of California Press.

Budiman, Abby, Luis Noe-Bustamante, and Mark Hugo Lopez. 2020. "Naturalized Citizens Make Up Record One-in-Ten U.S. Eligible Voters in 2020." Hispanic Trends. Washington, D.C.: Pew Research Center (February 26). https://www.pewresearch.org/hispanic/2020/02/26/naturalized-citizens-make-up-record-one-in-ten-u-s-eligible-voters-in-2020/.

Bush, Jeb, and Clint Bolick. 2013. *Immigration Wars: Forging an American Solution*. New York: Simon & Schuster.

Carey, John M., Gretchen Helmke, Brendan Nyhan, Mitchell Sanders, and Susan Stokes. 2019. "Searching for Bright Lines in the Trump Presidency." *Perspectives on Politics* 17(3, September): 699–718.

Carrigan, William, and Clive Webb. 2013. *Forgotten Dead: Mob Violence Against Mexicans in the United States, 1848–1928*. New York: Oxford University Press.

Carter, Shan, Jonathan Ellis, Farhana Hossain, and Alan McLean. 2008. "On the Issues: Immigration." *New York Times*, September 7. https://www.nytimes.com /elections/2008/president/issues/immigration.html.

Caruana, Nicholas J., R. Michael McGregor, and Laura B. Stephenson. 2015. "The Power of the Dark Side: Negative Partisanship and Political Behavior in Canada." *Canadian Journal of Political Science* 48(4, December): 771–89.

Cava, Marco della. 2020. "Latinos Disproportionately Dying, Losing Jobs Because of the Coronavirus: 'Something Has to Change.'" *USA Today*, April 18. https://www.usatoday.com/story/news/nation/2020/04/18 /coronavirus-latinos-disproportionately-dying-losing-jobs/5149044002/.

Citrin, Jack, and Laura Stoker. 2018. "Political Trust in a Cynical Age." *Annual Review of Political Science* 21: 49–70.

CNN News. 1993. "California Governor Discusses Illegal Immigration Plan." CNN, August 10.

Cohen, Marty, David Karol, Hans Noel, and John Zaller. 2008. *The Party Decides: Presidential Nominations Before and After Reform*. Chicago: University of Chicago Press.

Cohn, Nate. 2017. "The Upshot: Illegal Voting Claims, and Why They Don't Hold Up." *New York Times*, January 26. https://www.nytimes.com/2017/01/26/upshot /illegal-voting-claims-and-why-they-dont-hold-up.html.

Coyne, Tom. 2006. "Thousands at Indiana Rallies for Immigration Reform." *Associated Press*, April 11.

Crozier, Michel, Samuel P. Huntington, and Joji Watanuki. 1975. *The Crisis of Democracy*. New York: New York University Press.

C-SPAN Archives. 2013. "Senator Marco Rubio, (S. 744)." C-SPAN, June 11. https://www.c-span.org/video/?c4581992/sen-marco-rubio-62013.

D'Antonio, William, Steven Tuch, and Josiah Baker. 2013. *Religion, Politics, and Polarization: How Religiopolitical Conflict Is Changing Congress and American Democracy*. New York: Rowman and Littlefield.

Deng, Yiting, D. Sunshine Hillygus, Jerome P. Reiter, Yajuan Si, and Siyu Zheng. 2013. "Handling Attrition in Longitudinal Studies: The Case for Refreshment Samples." *Statistical Science* 28(2): 238–56.

Deville, Jean-Claude, Carl-Erik Sarnda, and Olivier Sautory. 1993. "Generalized Raking in Procedures in Survey Sampling." *Journal of the American Statistical Association* 88(423, September): 1013–20.

Dooling, Shannon. 2016. "Trump Election Spurs 'Panic' in Local Immigrant Communities." *WBUR Politicker*, November 15. https://www.wbur.org/politicker/2016/11/15 /trump-boston-immigrant-reaction.

Downs, Anthony. 1957. *An Economic Theory of Democracy.* New York: Harper & Row.

Dyck, Joshua, Gregg Johnson, and Jesse Wasson. 2012. "A Blue Tide in the Golden State." *American Politics Research* 40(3): 450–75.

Easton, David. 1965. *A Systems Analysis of Political Life.* New York: Wiley.

Eig, Larry M., and William J. Krouse. 1998. "Immigration: Adjustment to Permanent Residence Status Under Section 245(i)." Congressional Research Service Report for Congress, February 4. https://www.everycrsreport.com/reports/97-946.html.

Enchautegui, María E., and Linda Giannarelli. 2015. The *Economic Impact of Naturalization on Immigrants and Cities.* Washington, D.C.: Urban Institute (December). https://www.urban.org/sites/default/files/publication/76241/2000549-The-Economic-Impact-of-Naturalization-on-Immigrants-and-Cities.pdf.

Feldman, Stanley. 1982. "Economic Self-Interest and Political Behavior." *American Journal of Political Science* 26(3, August): 446–65.

Festinger, Leon. 1957. *A Theory of Cognitive Dissonance.* Palo Alto, Calif.: Stanford University Press.

Finkel, Steven E. 1995. *Causal Analysis with Panel Data.* Thousand Oaks, Calif.: Sage Publications.

Fraga, Luis R., John A. Garcia, Rodney Hero, Michael Jones-Correa, Valerie Martinez-Ebers, and Gary M. Segura. 2013. *Latino National Survey (LNS), 2006.* Ann Arbor, Mich.: Inter-university Consortium for Political and Social Research (distributor), June 5. DOI: 10.3886/ICPSR20862.v6.

Gomez, Brad T., and J. Matthew Wilson. 2006. "Cognitive Heterogeneity and Economic Voting: A Comparative Analysis of Four Democratic Electorates." *American Journal of Political Science* 50(1, January): 127–45.

Gulasekaram, Pratheepan, and Karthick Ramakrishnan. 2015. *The New Immigration Federalism.* New York: Cambridge University Press.

Gumbel, Andrew. 2016. "Doctors See a New Condition Among Immigrant Children: Fear of Trump." *Guardian*, November 25. https://www.theguardian.com/us-news/2016/nov/25/donald-trump-immigration-deportation-children-doctors.

Hacker, Jacob, and Paul Pierson. 2015. "Confronting Asymmetric Polarization." In *Solutions to Political Polarization in America,* edited by Nathaniel Persily. New York: Cambridge University Press.

Hainmueller, Jens, and Daniel Hopkins. 2014. "Public Attitudes Toward Immigration." *Annual Review of Political Science* 17: 225–49.

Hajnal, Zoltan, and Taeku Lee. 2011. *Why Americans Don't Join the Party: Race, Immigration, and the Failure (of Political Parties) to Engage the Electorate.* Princeton, N.J.: Princeton University Press.

Hayduk, Ron. 2006. *Democracy for All: Restoring Immigrant Voting Rights in the United States.* New York: Routledge.

Hetherington, Marc J. 2015. "Why Polarized Trust Matters." *The Forum* 13(3): 445–48.

Huddy, Leonie, Stanley Feldman, and Erin Cassese. 2007. "On the Distinct Political Effects of Anxiety and Anger." In *The Affect Effect: Dynamics of Emotion in Political Thinking and Behavior,* edited by W. Russell Neuman, George E. Marcus, Ann N. Crigler, and Michael MacKuen. Chicago: University of Chicago Press.

Huntington, Samuel P. 1981. *American Politics: The Promise of Disharmony*. Cambridge, Mass.: Harvard University Press.

Jones-Correa, Michael. 1998. *Between Two Nations*. Ithaca, N.Y.: Cornell University Press.

Jones-Correa, Michael, and David Leal. 1996. "Becoming 'Hispanic': Secondary Pan-Ethnic Identification among Latin American-Origin Populations in the United States." *Hispanic Journal of Behavioral Sciences* 18(2): 214–55.

Jones-Correa, Michael, and James A. McCann. 2013. "The Effects of Naturalization and Documentation Status on the Participation of Latino Immigrants." Paper presented at the annual meeting of the American Political Science Association. Chicago (August 28–September 1).

Jordan, Miriam, and Richard A. Oppel Jr. 2020. "For Latinos and Covid-19, Doctors Are Seeing an 'Alarming' Disparity." *New York Times*, May 7. https://www .nytimes.com/2020/05/07/us/coronavirus-latinos-disparity.html?referring Source=articleShare.

Kinder, Donald R., and Roderick Kiewiet. 1981. "Sociotropic Politics: The American Case." *British Journal of Political Science* 11(2, April): 129–61.

King, Gary, James Honaker, Anne Joseph O'Connell, and Kenneth Scheve. 2001. "Analyzing Incomplete Political Science Data: An Alternative Algorithm for Multiple Imputation." *American Political Science Review* 95(1, March): 49–69.

Koumpilova, Mila, and Faiza Mahamud. 2016. "Trump's Victory Triggers Anxiety Among Minnesota Somalis, Other Immigrants." *Star Tribune*, November 9. http://www.startribune.com/trump-s-victory-spurs-anxiety-for-local -somalis-and-other-immigrants/400610991/.

Kreis, Ramona. 2017. "The 'Tweet Politics' of President Trump." *Journal of Language and Politics* 16(4): 607–18.

Krogstad, Jens Manuel, Luis Noe-Bustamante, and Antonio Flores. 2019. "Historic Highs in 2018 Voter Turnout Extended Across Racial and Ethnic Groups." Washington, D.C.: Pew Research Center (May 1). https://www.pewresearch.org /fact-tank/2019/05/01/historic-highs-in-2018-voter-turnout-extended-across -racial-and-ethnic-groups/.

Kurtzleben, Danielle. 2016. "Do Americans Really Move to Canada Because of Politics?" National Public Radio, March 30. https://www.npr.org/2016/03/30/472279572 /do-americans-actually-follow-through-on-election-threats-to-move-to-canada.

Lamont, Michele, Bo Yun Park, and Elena Ayala-Hurtado. 2017. "Trump's Electoral Speeches and His Appeal to the American White Working Class." *British Journal of Sociology* 68(S1): S153–80.

Lau, Richard, and David Sears. 1981. "Cognitive Links Between Economic Grievances and Political Responses." *Political Behavior* 3(4): 279–302.

Lauter, David. 2012. "Central Issues of Election 2012: Data Desk." *Los Angeles Times*, October 13. https://timelines.latimes.com/central-issues-election-2012/.

Lawless, Jennifer L., and Richard Fox. 2018. "A Trump Effect? Women and the 2018 Midterm Elections." *The Forum* 16(4): 665–86.

Leal, David L. 2002. "Political Participation by Latino Non-Citizens in the United States." *British Journal of Political Science* 32(2): 353–70.

Leal, David L., Jerod Patterson, and Joe R. Tafoya. 2016. "Religion and the Political Engagement of Latino Immigrants: Bridging Capital or Segmented Religious Assimilation?" *RSF: The Russell Sage Foundation Journal of the Social Sciences* 2(3): 125–46. DOI: 10.7758/RSF.2016.2.3.07.

Lee, Michelle Ye Hee. 2015. "Donald Trump's False Comments Connecting Mexican Immigrants and Crime." *Washington Post*, July 8. https://www.washingtonpost.com /news/fact-checker/wp/2015/07/08/donald-trumps-false-comments-connecting -mexican-immigrants-and-crime/.

Lench, Heather C., Linda J. Levine, Kenneth Perez, Zari K. Haggenmiller, Steven J. Carlson, and Tom Tibbett. 2019. "Changes in Subjective Well-Being Following the U.S. Presidential Election of 2016." *Emotion* 19(1): 1–9.

Libell, Henrick Pryser, and Catherine Porter. 2018. "From Norway to Haiti, Trump's Comments Stir Fresh Outrage." *New York Times*, January 11. https:// www.nytimes.com/2018/01/11/world/trump-countries-haiti-africa.html.

Lofstrom, Magnus, Sarah Bohn, and Steven Raphael. 2011. "Lessons from the 2007 Legal Arizona Workers Act." San Francisco: Public Policy Institute of California (March). https://www.ppic.org/content/pubs/report/R_311MLR.pdf.

Lopez, Mark Hugo, Ana Gonzalez-Barrera, and Jens Manuel Krogstad 2018. "More Latinos Have Serious Concerns About Their Place in America Under Trump." Hispanic Trends. Washington, D.C.: Pew Research Center (October 25). https:// www.pewresearch.org/hispanic/2018/10/25/more-latinos-have-serious-concerns -about-their-place-in-america-under-trump/.

Lopez, Mark Hugo, Paul Taylor, Cary Funk, and Ana Gonzalez-Barrera. 2013. "On Immigration Policy, Deportation Relief Seen as More Important Than Citizenship." Hispanic Trends. Washington, D.C.: Pew Research Center (December 19). https://www.pewresearch.org/hispanic/2013/12/19/on-immigration-policy -deportation-relief-seen-as-more-important-than-citizenship/.

Madison, Lucy. 2012. "Romney on Immigration: I'm for 'Self-Deportation.'" CBS News, January 24. https://www.cbsnews.com/news/romney-on -immigration-im-for-self-deportation/.

Marcus, George, and Michael MacKuen. 1993. "Anxiety, Enthusiasm, and the Vote: The Emotional Underpinnings of Learning and Involvement During Presidential Campaigns." *American Political Science Review* 83(3, September): 672–85.

Marcus, George, Michael MacKuen, and W. Russell Neuman. 2000. *Affective Intelligence and Political Judgment*. Chicago: University of Chicago Press.

Martinez, Monica Muñoz. 2018. *The Injustice Never Leaves You: Anti-Mexican Violence in Texas*. Cambridge, Mass.: Harvard University Press.

Massey, Douglas S., Joaquín Arango, Graeme Hugo, Ali Kouauci, Adela Pellegrino, and J. Edward Taylor. 1993. "Theories of International Migration: A Review and Appraisal." *Population and Development Review* 19(3, September): 431–66.

Maxwell, Rahsaan. 2010. "Evaluating Migrant Integration: Political Attitudes Across Generations in Europe." *International Migration Review* 44(1, Spring): 25–52.

McCann, James A., and Michael Jones-Correa. 2016. "In the Public but Not the Electorate: The 'Civic Status Gap' in the United States." *RSF: The Russell Sage Foundation Journal of the Social Sciences* 3(2): 1–19. DOI: 10.7758/RSF.2016.2.3.01.

McCann, James A., David L. Leal, and Wayne A. Cornelius. 2009. "Absentee Voting and Transnational Civic Engagement Among Mexican Expatriates." In *Mexico's Choice: The 2006 Presidential Campaign in Comparative Perspective*, edited by Jorge Dominguez, Chappell Lawson, and Alejandro Moreno. Baltimore: Johns Hopkins University Press.

McCann, James A., and Katsuo A. Nishikawa Chávez. 2016. "Partisanship by Invitation: Immigrants Respond to Political Campaigns." *Journal of Politics* 78(4, August): 1196–1210.

Michelson, Melissa R. 2003. "The Corrosive Effect of Acculturation: How Mexican Americans Lose Political Trust." *Social Science Quarterly* 84(4, December): 918–33.

Miller, Claire Cain, and Kevin Quealy. 2017. "Democracy in America: How Is It Doing?" *New York Times*, February 23.

Min, Tae Eun. 2014. "The Impact of Panethnicity on Asian American and Latino Political Participation." *Ethnicities* 14(5, January): 698–721.

Monogan, James E. 2013. "The Politics of Immigrant Policy in the 50 U.S. States, 2005–2011." *Journal of Public Policy* 33(1): 35–64.

Morin, Jason L., Yoshira Macía Mejia, and Gabriel R. Sanchez. 2020. "Is the Bridge Broken? Increasing Ethnic Attachments and Declining Party Influence Among Latino Voters." *Political Research Quarterly*, first published online February 6. DOI: 10.1177/1065912919888577.

Muste, Christopher. 2013. "The Dynamics of Immigration Opinion in the United States, 1992–2012." *Public Opinion Quarterly* 77(1, Spring): 398–416.

National Academies of Sciences, Engineering, and Medicine. 2015. *The Integration of Immigrants into American Society*, edited by Mary Waters and Marisa Gerstein Pineau. Washington, D.C.: National Academies Press. DOI: 10.17226/21746.

Neuman, W. Russell, George E. Marcus, Ann N. Crigler, and Michael MacKuen, eds. 2007. *The Affect Effect: Dynamics of Emotion in Political Thinking and Behavior*. Chicago: University of Chicago Press.

Ngai, Mae. 2004. *Impossible Subjects: Illegal Aliens and the Making of Modern America*. Princeton, N.J.: Princeton University Press.

Norris, Pippa, ed. 1999. *Critical Citizens: Global Support for Democratic Government*. New York: Oxford University Press.

Pantoja, Adrian D., Cecilia Menjívar, and Lisa Magaña. 2008. "The Spring Marches of 2006: Latinos, Immigration, and Political Mobilization in the 21st Century." *American Behavioral Science* 57(4, December): 499–506.

Pantoja, Adrian, Ricardo Ramirez, and Gary Segura. 2001. "Citizens by Choice, Voters by Necessity." *Political Research Quarterly* 54(4, December): 729–50.

Parker, Christopher S. 2010. "Symbolic Versus Blind Patriotism." *Political Research Quarterly* 63(1): 97–114.

Pastor, Manuel, and Justin Scoggins. 2012. *Citizen Gain: The Economic Benefits of Naturalization for Immigrants and the Economy*. Los Angeles: University of Southern California, Center for the Study of Immigrant Integration (December). https://dornsife.usc.edu/csii/citizen-gain/.

Phoenix, Davin L. 2019. *The Anger Gap: How Race Shapes Emotion in Politics*. New York: Cambridge University Press.

Pierce, Sarah, Jessica Bolter, and Andrew Selee. 2018. "Trump's First Year on Immigration Policy: Rhetoric vs. Reality." Washington, D.C.: Migration Policy Institute (January). https://www.migrationpolicy.org/research/trump-first-year-immigration-policy-rhetoric-vs-reality.

Potochnick, Stephanie, and Mary Stegmaier. 2020. "Latino Political Participation by Citizenship Status and Immigrant Generation." *Social Science Quarterly* 101(2): 527–44.

Putnam, Robert. 2000. *Bowling Alone: The Collapse and Revival of American Community.* New York: Simon & Schuster.

Radford, Jynnah. 2019. "Key Findings About U.S. Immigrants." Washington, D.C.: Pew Research Center (June 17). https://www.pewresearch.org/fact-tank/2019/06/17/key-findings-about-u-s-immigrants/.

Redlawsk, David, and James A. McCann. 2005. "Popular Interpretations of 'Corruption' and Their Partisan Consequences." *Political Behavior* 27(3, September): 261–83.

Reich, Gary. 2018. "Hitting a Wall? The Trump Administration Meets Immigration Federalism." *Publius: The Journal of Federalism* 48(3, Summer): 372–95.

Reichel, David, and Laura Morales. 2017. "Surveying Immigrants Without Sampling Frames—Evaluating the Success of Alternative Field Methods." *Comparative Migration Studies* 5(1): 1–22.

Republican National Committee. 2015. *Growth & Opportunity Project.* Washington, D.C.: RNC (March). https://assets.documentcloud.org/documents/623664/republican-national-committees-growth-and.pdf.

Röder, Antje, and Peter Mühlau. 2011. "Discrimination, Exclusion, and Immigrants' Confidence in Public Institutions in Europe." *European Societies* 13(4): 535–57.

Rosenblum, Nancy. 2008. *On the Side of the Angels: An Appreciation of Parties and Partisanship.* Princeton, N.J.: Princeton University Press.

Rubin, Donald. 1987. *Multiple Imputation for Nonresponse in Surveys.* New York: J. Wiley & Sons.

Safire, William. 1992. *The First Dissident: The Book of Job in Today's Politics.* New York: Random House.

———. 1994. "Pete's Misery Index." *San Jose Mercury News*, November 22.

Schattschneider, E. E. 1969. *Two Hundred Million Americans in Search of a Government.* New York: Holt, Rinehart, and Winston.

———. 1975. *The Semisovereign People: A Realist's View of Democracy in America.* Hinsdale, Ill.: Dryden Press.

Schildkraut, Deborah. 2007. "Defining American Identity in the Twenty-First Century: How Much 'There' Is There?" *Journal of Politics* 69(3): 597–615.

Schlozman, Kay Lehman, Sidney Verba, and Henry E. Brady. 2012. *The Unheavenly Chorus: Unequal Political Voice and the Broken Promise of American Democracy.* Princeton, N.J.: Princeton University Press.

Sears, David O., Felix Danbold, and Vanessa M. Zavala. 2016. "Incorporation of Latino Immigrants into the American Party System." *RSF: The Russell Sage Foundation Journal of the Social Sciences* 2(3): 182–204. DOI: 10.7758/RSF.2016.2.3.10.

Shames, Shauna L. 2017. *Out of the Running: Why Millennials Reject Political Careers and Why It Matters.* New York: New York University Press.

Shear, Michael, and Trip Gabriel. 2012. "In Speech, Romney Takes Softer Tone on Immigration." *New York Times*, June 21. https://thecaucus.blogs.nytimes.com/2012/06/21/romney-outlines-approach-to-immigration-in-speech-to-latino-officials/.

Sides, John, Michael Tesler, and Lynn Vavreck. 2018a. "Hunting Where the Ducks Are: Activating Support for Donald Trump in the 2016 Republican Primary." *Journal of Elections, Public Opinion, and Parties* 28(2): 135–56.

———. 2018b. *Identity Crisis: The 2016 Presidential Campaign and the Battle for the Meaning of America.* Princeton, N.J.: Princeton University Press.

Somerville, Will, Jamie Durana, and Aaron Matteo Terrazas. 2008. "Hometown Associations: An Untapped Resource for Immigrant Integration?" *Migration Policy Institute Insight* (July). https://www.migrationpolicy.org > pubs > Insight-HTAs-July08.

Sullivan, J. L., and J. E. Transue. 1999. "The Psychological Underpinnings of Democracy: A Selective Review of Research on Political Tolerance, Interpersonal Trust, and Social Capital." *Annual Review of Psychology* 50: 625–50.

Tenpas, Kathryn Dunn, James A. McCann, and Emily J. Charnock. 2018. "Trump Makes Fewer Public Trips than Recent Presidents. Will That Hurt the Republicans in November?" *Washington Post*, January 17. https://www.washingtonpost.com/news/monkey-cage/wp/2018/01/17/trump-makes-fewer-public-trips-than-recent-presidents-will-that-hurt-the-republicans-in-november/.

Theiss-Morse, Elizabeth. 2009. *Who Counts as an American? The Boundaries of National Identity.* New York: Cambridge University Press.

Tolchin, Susan J. 1999. *The Angry American: How Voter Rage Is Changing the Nation.* Boulder, Colo.: Westview Press.

Tyler, Tom R. 1990. *Why People Obey the Law.* Princeton, N.J.: Princeton University Press.

Uhlaner, Carole, Bruce Cain, and D. Roderick Kiewiet. 1989. "Political Participation of Ethnic Minorities in the 1980s." *Political Behavior* 11(3): 195–231.

Valdez, Carmen R., Jessa L. Valentine, and Brian Padilla. 2013. "'Why We Stay': Immigrants' Motivations for Remaining in Communities Impacted by Anti-Immigration Policy." *Cultural Diversity and Ethnic Minority Psychology* 19(3): 279–87.

Valentino, Nicholas A., Ted Brader, Eric W. Groenendyk, Krysha Gregorowicz, and Vincent Hutchings. 2011. "Election Night's Alright for Fighting: The Role of Emotions in Political Participation." *Journal of Politics* 73(1, January): 156–70.

Valentino, Nicholas A., Vincent Hutchings, Antoine Banks, and Anne Davis. 2008. "Is a Worried Citizen a Good Citizen? Emotions, Political Information Seeking, and Learning via the Internet." *Political Psychology* 29(2, April): 247–73.

Verba, Sidney, Kay Lehman Schlozman, and Henry E. Brady. 1995. *Voice and Equality: Civic Voluntarism in American Politics.* Cambridge, Mass.: Harvard University Press.

Wallace, Sophia, Michael Jones-Correa, and Chris Zepeda-Millán. 2016. "The Impact of Large-Scale Collective Action on Latino Perceptions of Commonality and Competition with African-Americans." *Social Science Quarterly* 97(2, May): 458–75.

Wampler, Brian, Maria Chávez, and Francisco I. Pedraza. 2009. "Should I Stay or Should I Go? Explaining Why Most Mexican Immigrants Are Choosing to Remain Permanently in the United States." *Latino Studies* 7(1): 83–104.

Warren, Mark. 2017. "What Kinds of Trust Does a Democracy Need?" In *Handbook on Political Trust*, edited by Sonja Zmerli and Tom W. G. Van der Meer. Cheltenham, U.K.: Edward Elgar.

Warren, Robert. 2020. "Reverse Migration to Mexico Led to U.S. Undocumented Population Decline: 2010–2018." *Journal on Migration and Human Security* 8(1): 32–41.

Washington Post (staff). 2015. "Full Text: Donald Trump Announces a Presidential Bid." *Washington Post*, June 16. https://www.washingtonpost.com/news/post-politics/wp/2015/06/16/full-text-donald-trump-announces-a-presidential-bid/.

Watson, David, and Auke Tellegen. 1985. "Toward a Consensual Structure of Mood." *Psychological Bulletin* 98(2): 219–35.

Wilkes, Rima, and Cary Wu. 2018. "Trust and Minority Groups." In *The Oxford Handbook of Social and Political Trust*, edited by Eric M. Uslaner. New York: Oxford University Press.

Wong, Janelle. 2006. *Democracy's Promise: Immigrants and American Civic Institutions.* Ann Arbor: University of Michigan Press.

Wroe, Andrew. 2008. *The Republican Party and Immigration Politics: From Proposition 187 to George W. Bush.* New York: Palgrave Macmillan 2008.

Zaller, John, and Stanley Feldman. 1992. "A Simple Theory of the Survey Response: Answering Questions Versus Revealing Preferences." *American Journal of Political Science* 36(3, August): 579–616.

Zepeda-Millán, Chris. 2017. *Latino Mass Mobilization: Immigration, Racialization, and Activism.* New York: Cambridge University Press.

Zúñiga, Victor, and Rubén Hernández-León, eds. 2005. *New Destinations: Mexican Immigration in the United States.* New York: Russell Sage Foundation.

INDEX

Boldface numbers refer to figures and tables.